# When Lilacs were in Bloom

By DAROLD 'DICK' FREDRICKS

First Edition

Published by
Rushmore House Publishing
Box 1591
Sioux Falls, South Dakota 57101



Cover photo: 1935 Fredricks family collection (FF Collection)
Title Page photo: Washington High School in the 1950s.
(Charles Fredricks)

ISBN: 0-9624593-8-0

LCCN: 99-76181

Printed by Pine Hill Press, Inc.,
Sioux Falls, South Dakota

## DEDICATED

TO MY LOVING WIFE, PEGGY FREDRICKS,
AND MY CHILDREN, KIM AND KAROL,
ALL OF WHOM NEVER COMPLAINED
AS THEY LISTENED TO
AND ENDURED FOR COUNTLESS YEARS
THE MANY STORIES THAT ARE IN THIS BOOK.

LILAC—n. Bluish (indigo) dark blue, indigo; any group of hardy shrubs or trees with large clusters of tiny, fragrant flowers—ranging in color from white, through many shades of lavender, to deep crimson.

*Webster New World Dictionary 1962*

———— or any group of hardy people, with large clusters of tiny, fragrant children—ranging in size from small to large.

*Special thanks to my wife Peggy Fredricks and my friend George de Shazer for their help on this book.*

# Table of Contents

# Introduction

*When Lilacs Were in Bloom* by Darold 'Dick' Fredricks is a series of vignettes that reveal the life and times of a midwestern family in the 1930s and 1940s. The Fredricks family, as well as many other families, strived to remain intact during trying economic times, and at the same time pass on their family values to their children. These values were crucial to my life especially after 1944 when my mother died and I struggled to 'find' my way in the world. The most important part of my life revolved around school—high school and college. After completing my college degree at Augustana in 1957, I decided that the degrees that I had struggled to attain could not be fully utilized in the Heartland. I looked to greener pastures in California and took a teaching job in the San Francisco Bay area..

The Midwest had well-prepared me for my coaching and teaching career in California. As I look back on my life in Sioux Falls from the perspective of California, I realize what a good foundation I had gained for my life.

In the 30s and 40s life was not a 'Leave It to Beaver' type of existence as depicted in the T.V. series. In the classroom I would sometimes find myself explaining my life in the Midwest to my students, contrasting the present with the past. This added a great deal of interest to my students, as they realized that I had had to struggle much as many of them had. Although my life seemed cruel and harsh much of the time while growing up, my father strove to maintain his job and his dignity, and at the same time instill in me hope that things could be better. At the same time I did not feel that he had become cynical because of the lack of funds he felt we needed but he could not earn.

**The Depression was not a brief affair. It persisted for many, many years and molded the attitudes, spending habits, and ideals of millions of children during this decade.**

In spite of the economic gloom cast over the country, children's lives persisted and flourished. Outwardly they accepted much of the situation, as they had not known any other conditions and they lived out their childhood as if the world were normal.

***When Lilacs Were in Bloom* is a series of vignettes of my childhood in Sioux Falls. My curiosity was unending, my play was innovative among the railroad tracks close to home; my trips to Drake Springs, shoveling snow, riding bicycles, 'running' the neighborhood, walking to school, climbing trees and adjusting to the quiet and peacefulness of the lower-class neighborhood I grew up in molded my life.**

These vignettes are glimpses into the 1930s using my eyes and ears and my special perception of a child's world.

Life was full of hope for me. However, my ultimate disaster occurred when my mother died when I was eleven years old. This event changed my life forever. It made me bitter for a time, but eventually I recovered and my inherent desire and drive pushed me on to higher heights of achievements.

Washington High School gave me a new "lease on life" after my mother died. The new friendships I made there and winning the Eastern South Dakota championship in 1950 while on the football team in my senior year gave me the confidence I needed to face the world.

Much of my success I now feel can be attributed to the wonderful acquaintances and friends that surrounded me during my life in the Heartland. I have tried to give some of them credit for my life in the listing found in this book. Actually, I discovered the longer I was away from the Heartland the more I thought of the 'roots' I had developed as a child and this led me to writing down these wonderful experiences so I could share them with friends and my children.

*Going to take a sentimental journey..................*

# 1

# The Beginning........East Side

The red-haired young woman stared out the second-floor window and watched as her man climbed into a truck and started it. A sign on the door of the truck indicated 'Parmley Coal'. He closed the door, rolled down the window, stuck his hand out and waved to her. She waved back and continued to watch the truck as it moved slowly down to the corner and disappeared. She watched as if it were still visible, but she knew it would not return until the end of the day, twelve hours away. Slowly her hands pressed against her body and she ran them down the length of her dress, as if caressing it until they felt the bulge of the forming baby.

She felt old. It had been only ten years last June since she and Elmer had eloped in Canton. She hadn't been in a family way then, she just loved him and wanted to be with him but she didn't want their parents to know about their marriage at that time. Their first baby, born a year after they eloped, had lived only three days. However, a healthy girl born a year and a half later had made up for this great loss to her. It was two years before a boy was born. This was followed by a beautiful girl two years later. A boy, Charles was born next, and now she was pregnant again. This strain of childbearing was beginning to show in her face and she was continually tired now. Five children in ten years, and now another one on the way. She still loved her husband, but the strain of his trying to keep them fed and clothed, not to mention paying rent, was taking a toll on their marriage. If only this fellow, Roosevelt, could get some more jobs for the working man, things would be different for them. Only time would tell....

The trees looked so fresh and green this early in the morning, she thought. Before long they would lose their green color, turn bright golden browns and yellows and began to fall. 'I like mornings', she said to herself. They are so peaceful and full of hope. The shadows had begun to form under the trees as the sun rose higher and scattered its light everywhere. She could hear movements below in the grocery store and knew Mr. Jenkins and his wife would be eating breakfast soon, before they opened for the day. All that food! So close and yet so far away and so much need for it up here. She turned as a youngster, a sleepy-eyed girl, appeared at the kitchen table and pulled herself up to it. The girl had dropped her 'night-night' blanket on the floor before she climbed up the high-backed chair.

"Is Daddy at work now?" she asked.

"Yes, he just left in the truck for another day's work with Mr. Parmley. Looks like a full day today for him, aren't you glad?"

"Does he have to deliver coal all day today?"

"Yes, all day today."

The two large rooms of the apartment had been partitioned off to make an additional room, but it was still crowded with the baby crib, bed and sofa that two children slept on. There was one other set of blankets on the floor where the older boy had slept and had to be stepped over when the children were sleeping. The kitchen was now a welcome relief from the crowdedness of the other rooms.

'We've got to get some more room for the kids, Elmer,' she had told him. 'With the baby coming soon, we have no more room to move around in. We've got to look for something else and get out of this second-floor apartment. It isn't right for the kids. There is no place to play, or anything. I'm going crazy living like this above the grocery store. We need to look for something else, a house, or a farm, but we can't stay here.'

"If I keep my job at the coal yard, we could probably find something. There's talk of layoffs after this month unless we get more orders for coal. Damn gas stoves are being put in now that natural gas is available and the boss says orders are down quite a bit. I'll ask around, maybe we can move after this semester is over for the kids."

"Well, let's start looking around because we need to do something before long."

..............................

"Go get Mommy, I'm ready now." Ruby excitedly shouted to Elmer as she gasped for breath, taking short pants of breath to get more air. "I've been having pain off and on for the last hour and it won't be too long before it comes. Hurry. They say the sixth one is the fastest...and the easiest, so get along fast." She lay back down exhausted on the neatly made-up bed, with the pain showing in her face. 'Oh, I hope this one is easy,' she thought to herself. 'What would the kids do if anything happened to me now?'

"Dorothy, quick, run and ask Mrs. Jenkins to come up and watch the other kids until Grandma gets here." Elmer spoke as he hurriedly put on his heavy black broadcloth coat. He opened the door that led down the back stairs to his truck, shouting to Mrs. Jenkins in the grocery store that the time was near.

He now wished that he had a telephone. Oh, what he would give for a telephone right now, but he knew it cost a nickel to use the one in the store. So, he kept going toward the truck, angry at himself that he didn't have the money for the telephone. She'd be all right when her mother gets here to help her have the baby. Other than the first child which died after three days of life, all of her births had been easy and fast. All but the first. That child had lived only three days before she died. The death was felt deeply by everyone, but there would be more.

The sixth is said to be the easiest, Ruby thought to herself, and if there were any complications her mother would know what to do and, if needed, Aunt Helen would come over later when she found out about the birth.. Aunt Helen was the nurse of the family and she was around when needed after all the childbirths. Well, she wasn't exactly a real nurse, but she knew what to do when somebody was ailing. The family could always depend on her. By tomorrow she would have everything under control in the household. She would cook meals, wash and mend clothes, and bathe children. She was an angel. Without her, he didn't know what he would have done over the years. Her heart was too big sometimes and she gave too much of herself, but that was the way she did things in her life.

..............................

The ground was frozen. It was very cold, below zero, and he slapped his hands together as he ran toward the truck door and began fumbling for his keys for the ignition. The ignition on, the truck engine turned over slowly one time, then two times....

"Damn it! Start. Don't die on me now." He turned the switch off for a second before he turned it on again. Over it turned again, and when he was almost ready to quit, it roared to life for a second. "Come on now, don't fail me." he said as he turned the key in the ignition again and pumped the accelerator to get more gasoline into the carburetor. This time it turned faster and started with a roar. He quickly adjusted the choke, trying to keep it going. This time it continued to run and he sat there on the cold seat waiting until he felt it had warmed up enough. Putting it into gear, he charged out onto the street and headed for Grandma's house.

On that cold, cold winter night in February their sixth child was brought into this world, crying to high heaven as if resisting its very entry into the world. The birth had been uneventful, everything looked normal. He weighted six pounds, seven ounces and was born with a hunger that would last the rest of his life.

..............................

The cold, brutal South Dakota winter kept on. The food bills mounted, clothes were worn and re-worn although they should have been thrown away, and out of the clear blue sky, Elmer found out that the rent was to be raised.

"I can't afford any more rent," he said to Ruby as they lay in bed. It was time to move to another place and hope for the best with a new landlord.

With five mouths to feed, plus himself and his wife, sixteen dollars a week did not go far.

Father had been born and raised in a small town in Nebraska. His family moved to this river town in Nebraska after the fields of Northern Missouri quit providing enough food for the family to live on. Grandpa Charles' large family and his parents who lived with him also needed cash for staples such as clothes, shoes, and the food they could not grow. Cash was scarce in the Missouri town of Coffee. The farm that Grandpa Charles had put his hopes in to provide his livelihood never worked out. There were too many mouths to feed and more children would be expected to arrive as he was still a young man.

A horse race track had just been built in the town of Ponka so he just pulled up his roots in Missouri and took off in search of his dream—a cash-paying job at the race track.

It was not to be. Again he fell on tough times. The work and money he expected didn't pan out, so after admitting another failure, he again packed his family and worldly goods on the train after taking a ferry across the waters of the Missouri at Elk Point.

Father was attending the fifth grade in school and he was ten years old at the time of this trip to South Dakota. He had been pulled out of school when he left Ponka and he never went back to school after that, a decision he later regretted.

Grandpa Fredricks rented a farm on the bluffs of the Sioux River, to the south of the bustling city of 14,000 people,Sioux Falls.

The farm needed the hands of youth to do the chores that kept a farm going. Elmer and his brothers supplied those hands. Diligence, hard work, pugnacity, and thrift were virtues taught him by his parents. The following eight years were spent working on this farm a mile south of the Big Sioux River and on a farm situated to the north of the Big Sioux on the opposite side of town. Grandpa and Grandma continued to live with them on these two farms. Grandpa could still read the Bible without glasses. His legs were still able to carry him to Riverside for tobacco and groceries. One by one the brothers married and moved away. Finally, in 1918, the family gave up on farming and moved into the town that had grown to 25,000. They settled down to the city life.

The war in Europe was raging in the late1910s but my father never participated in it. One of his older brothers, Frank, joined and was gassed by the Germans with mustard gas while in France. He lingered on for ten years, half alive and half dead before dying of his war injuries.

With the war over, America turned inward to search for its identity as the rest of the world went on its way.

America was just emerging as an industrial giant, but the fruits of the revolution had not yet filtered into the Heartland of America and good employment was difficult to find, especially for a twenty-year old farm boy with a fifth-grade education. Menial labor, however, was always in demand, even though it paid almost no money. Such was the fate of a child with little education in a economy with millions of workers. Jobs such as driving trucks or delivering coal to houses were occasionally found, but did not prove to be full-time occupations. The drifting and infrequent employment did not allow him to save much money or develop any skills that would advance his employment. He continued to live at his parents' home on Third Avenue and was living there when he met Ruby Lane. Ruby was living with her parents on the East Side of Sioux Falls. A whirlwind courtship resulted in a marriage that they did not reveal until a year after it had happened. He continued living with his parents and Ruby lived with her mother, until her pregnancy became obvious.

..............................

The days began getting longer. The dark nights and overcast, moody days were becoming fewer and fewer. Spring was definitely on its way. The mood of the family changed with the weather and the sun shone bright and clear. Change was in the air. A few months after the blond-haired boy named Fred was born, the family moved. Elmer had found a house that offered a better place for them to live.

"Found a house over by McKennan Hospital, on Eighth Avenue, Ruby. Why don't we take a look at it this weekend? It is cheaper and it has a yard and a garden area that can be planted. The land where we can put in a garden is a whole lot. It'll help out with the food bill. The builder of the house has decided to leave the big city and return to Hartford and begin farming again after having lived here for only a few years. You know, he told me the city had grown to over 33,000 people. The big city life doesn't appeal to him anymore. The town's getting too crowded, he says."

That Sunday they piled the family into the truck he had brought home from work, and drove over to the house.

"Ruby, it's all we can afford. Someday we'll get a bigger one, but for now, it will have to do," he apologized.

"It'll be just fine, Father. We can make it a fine home. It's a good house, Elmer, don't fret. It will do." And she meant it, although she had hoped they would be able to have indoor plumbing. Maybe in the next home, she confided to herself, but for now it was a beautiful house.

After living in a two-room apartment above a grocery store, this house looked like a palace to her. Elmer knew a good business deal when he saw it, so he rented the house for $15 a month. To my father, this was a week's salary, as the hard times of the depression barely afforded a living wage for anyone. 'Take it or leave it' his boss had said as he cut his wage from $25 to $15 only a few months before. Times were hard and he was happy to have any job at the moment.

..............................

*In the late 1920's there were two children in the family. (FF Collection)*

The jobs dried up in the Midwest. Something to do with the stock market, they had heard. They called it a depression. And it did not go away. The depression continued to be with the country and it bit deeper and deeper into the psyche and the pocketbook of America. The president said it would go away, but he was voted out and a new president, President Roosevelt, said he would straighten out the county. However, he had more trouble than he had thought he would have, and the country continued in the doldrums. There still were very few new jobs being created, not enough for the millions of unemployed. The Government finally responded to the voices of the millions of the destitute and began creating jobs cleaning up and rebuilding the internal structure of the Country in a Government agency called the W.P.A. No longer did millions of unemployed have to stand in soup lines to get their only meal of the day, they could now regain some of their lost dignity by performing labor for which they were paid cash. In Germany a man called

Hitler was gaining more power throughout Europe as he fed on fear of the millions who became disappointed with the political system.

President Roosevelt promised a new era in America now that Social Security would be available to the working man.

*Brother can you spare a dime?.............*

*Hauling coal was common in the 20's and Dad was good at his job. (FF Collection)*

# Sioux Falls People

Daryl Abbey • Bud Adams • Eugene Adamson • Nettie Adler • Rose Albert • Deane Robert Aldern • Tom Bob Amburn • Dee Amos • Bob Anderson • Don Anderson • Wallace Anderson • Kenny Anderson • Helen Anderson • Courtney Anderson • Earl Angle • DeEtta Anderberg • Lois Antrim • Joe Artman • Ralph Esther Bailey • Burl Baker • Roger Bakke • Betty Ball • Russ Ball • Dale Barnhart • Vernon Barck • Lorraine Barnes • Don Bartholow • Mitzi Baustian • Bob Dick Beck • C. R. Beck • R. A. Beck • Bonnie Beck • Pete Beckman • James Bell • Al Benson • Oliver Robert Berg • Carol Berg • Bob Berguin • Lillan Sachen Berreth • Margaret Sunderman Berrett • Gwen Bertelsen • Ted Harvey Al Edward Earl Marv Kevin Francis Beuckens • Brad Brian Beuckens • Marie Wilcox Bingen • Bob Bissell • Bob Bittner • Elta Nelson Tom Beverly Frank Vandendale Norma George Eingher Doris Douglas Jeffery Dona Laura Black • Leonard Blackburn • Gloria Gulbrandson Block • Dick Bob Blue • Ray Bly • Daniel Louisa Harry Clara Mable Eva Della Minnie Ruth Verea William Sarah Earl William Betty Gall Glen Viola Russell Bonacker • Dorothy Boersma • Newman Booker • Dick Bowen • Florence Braa • Mare Caldwell Bradley • Harlen June Fredricks Linda Hebert Diane Moberly Wendell Kenneth Russell Jeffrey Brandt • Linda Tracy Shawn Chad Miranda Cole Hebert Diane Matthew Meghan Moberly Wendell Patricia Nathan Lindsey Brandt • Kenneth Gayle Sebbo Jamie Jessica Christopher Martha Warsing Jenny David Jessica Brandt • Russell Candy Wahl Brandt • Jeffrey Brandt • Harriet Branson • Deanna Brewer • Norma Brewer • Rudi Brewster • Evelyn Brandsgaard Bridenstine • Beverly Brown • Don Brown • Evelyn Norman Nancy Billy Brown • Keith Brown • John Brusninghan • Bill Bubbers • Peggy Buck • Darlene Hoefert Buckley • Darlene Budgett • Gloria Tracy Bultena • Len Robert Tim Burhenn • Don Burk • Carol Burke • Irene Fred Butler Robert Bott Barbara Jean Bott Fines David Butler Roger Alyce Butler Dale Holly Butler • Ruth Butts • Don Buxton • Stan Cadwell • Marilyn Harmer Marge Bradley Joanna Jocelyn Caldwell • Doris Linda Cain • Betty Campbell • Bob Carlson • Carrie Lane Ed Homer Faye Roger John Carol Ella Victor Carlson • Bob Carlson • Emil Rose Carlson • Roger Carnahan • Fern Chamberlain • Lloyd Fern Doris Bob Postma Floyd Glen Betty Knock Bonnie Conklin Lawrence Robert Chambers • Francis Chase • Mary Cheney • Dorothy Elmen Christensen • Richard Christensen • Bob Christianson • Sally Christenson • Chris Christopolos • Alvina Clark • Clinton Clark • Howie Clark • Ron Clark • Fritz Clements • Edna Monger Colwill • Robin Coon • Lorraine Hayes Sybil Hayes Irene Schurman Windy Bonnie Chambers Conklin • Betty Sachen Coulter • *(continued on page 28)*

# 2
# Eighth Avenue Home

The day was bright and breezy as the hard-tired truck that belonged to his boss, with all of their life's belongings, furniture, clothes, and kids in it, slowly moved across the eight bumpy railroad tracks of the Great Northern Railroad. Their destination could be seen only a block away. Elmer shifted the truck into low gear so as not to jostle the kids and furniture around too much on the rough railroad tracks. Automatically he looked up and down the tracks for signs of a train. There was none coming and he again concentrated on the road.

"Have to get the kids up here later to find some fire wood from the empty railroad cars they store along here," Dad said. "Sometimes they leave a lot of wood in them, and sometimes other things. Looks like some coal along the tracks could be gathered for the stove." He paused as if to make a proclamation. In low gear he drove down the dirt road, slowed down even further, and carefully turned south onto Eighth Avenue. The truck lurched as he pulled off the road. The kids let out a scream.

"Here we are, everybody out," he shouted, but the kids were already piling out of the truck's bed. "Hey, come back here" he yelled. "Help me get the stuff off of the truck." Too late. All that could be seen were their backs. Their swift little feet carried them in every direction of the yard and away from the truck. Their exuberance told all.

"It's beautiful, Elmer." Ruby said as she looked at their new home. "It's going to be a good place to live in. Look at those trees. It has trees, space, and a yard. **A YARD.** My lord, look at the size of the yard."

Yard! that's pushing the definition a bit much. There was plenty of space, both in the front and the back. However, there was no grass growing anywhere, only weeds.

"Those weeds need to be cut soon," Dad said as he got out of the truck, "or we'll lose one or two of the kids in them. I don't have time to form a search party to find lost kids right now with all I have to do," he chuckled.

The small, one-story, wooden-framed structure that Dad had stopped in front of sparkled in the sunlight. It was painted white. It sat on a large corner, back from the road. The house had two porches that she could see: a shallow porch in the front facing Eighth Avenue, on the east side, and a small screened-in porch on the north side. It would be nice sitting out on the porch at night, she thought. So restful after a full day. Bordering the house were the wide dirt-lined streets of Seventeenth Street and Eighth Avenue.

"Let them run for a while. We can get the things in time," he shouted back as he walked toward a big vacant lot on the south side of the house.

He stopped, returned to the cab of the truck and spoke, "Look at all of the room we'll have, Mother. Finally a bedroom just for us, think of it, just for us. Mother just sat and looked out from the the truck, watching the children. The two oldest children, Norman and Dorothy were spotted as they ran pell-mell across the vacant lot to the south of the house, before they spied the crab apple tree and took off for it. Dorothy ran to the truck.

"Hey, look, Mommy, a crab apple tree. When they're ripe, can I have one? Can I?"

Mom looked in the direction of the tree. "That won't be for a few months, but we'll see. Maybe I can make some jelly from the apples. How would you like that?"

Mommy sat in the truck and looked at the house. A palace, she thought...and it's theirs. Finally she would have a house with a yard.

It was a neat looking house, she thought. The trim painted the same color as the wooden sides—white. Around the base of the house the pink paper used for winter insulation was still nailed to the house. Have to get Dad to take that off, she thought to herself. The front door was screened to keep flies out. The porch looked onto Eighth Avenue. She turned her head and looked across the street at the two-story white house that sat there. Nice looking. An older white-haired lady was looking out the front porch windows, and when she saw Ruby looking, she waved. Ruby waved back. She got out of the truck, reached back and picked up a blanket with Fred in it, and walked toward the back of the house. She passed the apple tree and stood about ten feet from the house and looked over the back area. There she saw a small wooden porch leading to the back door. This'll be what we'll probably use most, she said. Who needs a front door? It isn't friendly.

A couple of ten-foot-tall elm trees were growing in the back yard. Her eyes swept across the yard and rested on a bush. A lilac bush. Trees as well as a lilac bush that was beginning to bud—she almost cried. A lilac tree! I've always wanted my own lilac tree—and trees to sit under. What a change.

Overgrown with weeds and with patches of dirt visible, the back yard showed very little evidence of upkeep by the previous occupants. There was a well-worn path leading through the weeds to the outdoor privy, however. Glancing north, across the street there was a two-story house with two youngsters watching the group with intensity. Ruby waved to them and they waved back shyly.

."Now I'll have a place to put the car to keep it out of the weather. Can keep my tools out there also." Dad proudly pointed out the garage to the oldest boy, Norman. The back of the property abutted onto the neighbor's back yard where a garden being prepared for the planting of vegetables could be seen.

"Look at the space, Mother." Elmer said as he looked around the back yard. To the south of the house was an empty lot. A nice big garden could be put in here.

Pushing his black pompadour back on his head he moved toward the vacant lot. "Here we can raise tomatoes, string beans, onions, radishes, peas, potatoes, beets, carrots, sweet corn, and watermelons, Mother. This'll be great." Elmer exclaimed. "Fresh vegetables. We'll can what we don't eat right away. Should have enough food for all winter long. The kids can help keep it weeded and whenever we need vegetables, all we have to do is go to the garden and pick them. Look at all of the room we have to plant. Have to get someone to plow it for us come spring, but that can wait for now." He walked toward the front porch, and, as he walked he looked at the weeds and spoke to Ruby. "I'll have to do something about these weeds. Need to borrow a scythe first from Frank. I know he has one. If I had a phone I could call him before he comes over this afternoon. Well, it can wait until tomorrow. Lot of things to do now that we have a house." He turned and walked toward the back door of the house. "Come on, Mother. Let's take a look."

Dad opened the door and entered. The kitchen was just inside the door.

Along the wall stood a porcelain sink. A 'walk-in' food and storage closet could be seen along the opposite wall.

"Mom, the sink works," said Dorothy with surprise as she turned on the faucet. She had already tested it while dad and ma were in the back yard. The sink boasted incoming city water, but the water from the sink ran to the side of the house through a pipe where it flowed onto the ground.

"Dorothy, turn it off. Don't waste the water," she admonished her. "We have to pay for it now."

"The washing machine will have to be put into the kitchen for now," Mother told Elmer. "We may have to use part of the kitchen for the boys' bedroom," he spoke as he looked around. He stepped into the adjoining room and continued speaking, "The front room would be just right for our table. Not much room for chairs and sitting." He kept looking around.

"Maybe we can move the kitchen out here into the dining room, whatever you want to call it, and redo the kitchen for the boys," she said. "Leave the sink there, it's close enough. Put the stove here in the dining room. Put the small table in here also, and we can eat in the front room." Secretly she had wanted a dining room for the large table, but that was all right. A dining room could wait. The kids had to be taken care of first.

Elmer looked at her in amazement. Just what he had thought. That solves the problem, and he didn't have to suggest all of the solutions. "The boys can sleep out on the porch until I get it done."

"Yes, they'll be okay on the side porch for now."

This two-bedroom apartment-sized house was to become home to my two older brothers, two older sisters, and my mother and father. In it was a den-sized bedroom for my sisters, one 'master bedroom' for the parents, a living room that was used as a bedroom at times, a small front room, and a kitchen.

The kids ran into the house. With every footstep, the room echoed loudly with the sound of hard-soled shoes on bare wood. Empty of furniture, every room became an echo chamber as the kids ran from room to room looking into everything and yelling with delight. Every opened door was a new discovery.

"Look in here," one of the girls exclaimed as she entered a small room.

"Keep your voices down. That's enough of that. The neighbors will think we have a tribe of Indians over here," said Dad as he grabbed the nearest one and subdued him. The other three immediately ground to a halt and put their hands over their mouths in mock silence.

"That'll be your room, girls. Get your stuff and put it in there," Dad said as he pointed to a small room that was just large enough for one bed. It had a few built-in shelves on the south wall that could be used for clothes and toys. The girls ran for the front door. Dad turned to Ruby. "The girls can use this bedroom, Mother. We'll put their things in here right now and set up the bed."

"We'll get our bed and put it in here," Elmer said as he pointed to a room between the girls' east-facing room and the kitchen. This was to be the parents' 'master bedroom". "It won't be so bad, Mother," he said as he put his arm around her. "It will be our sanctuary." Here at the end of the day, they would finally be able to escape from the children and live the joys of man and wife. This room was not to be entered by the children or hidden in when playing hide-and-seek. This was the parents' room.

Upon entering the front door, one encountered a small vestibule with sliding doors between it and what was to have been a 'formal' dining room. There was not enough room for the family for use as a 'formal' dining room and this became the main center of living in the house. Here, in the evening, dolls were played with, cards were played. Later when a radio was bought, it was listened to by the entire family who sat around in chairs or laid on the cold, hard floor. With rapt attention everyone listened as 'Fibber Magee and Molly' blared out into the night.

In the middle of the dining room there was a new addition to the home... and soon to become the centerpiece of the home...the table. This table was special. It was oval, with four large lion-paw legs giving it stability.The table had seen better days, but it still had a lot of character. Three- and a-half feet wide, six feet long, it sat squarely in the center of the room, proclaiming its position in the life of the family. Now it was bare. Sunday would be the day when it would be in its glory. Then it would be covered with a tablecloth, maybe linen, but more often common cloth. There was room enough for ten chairs around it if all of the leaves were put in and the chairs were squeezed together. The original brown stain of its boards had long faded and been replaced with new stain many times. Stain that somehow didn't quite cover it as beautifully as the original had. The stain was streaked, and showed the wear of the thousands of meals that had been lovingly served and gratefully consumed around its perimeter. The table was made of oak. Iron was what was needed to help make it last all of its life, but oak had been chosen. It was built to last the ages, and to serve the families that would need it. Large families, small families, individuals, groups of two or three. It would sit there in the middle of the room as if its only duty was to wait and serve.

Grandma had it before giving it to the family. Her family was gone now. Buried. And she was waiting for her end. It was no longer needed by her, so she gave it to her son...and his family. To use. It needed to be used. It was such a lovely piece of furniture, she had said, as it was loaded onto the truck by her son. It was his now. It took its place in the center of a new room, and began a new life for the new family.

*Grab your coat, and get your hat leave your worries on the doorstep Just direct your feet To the sunny side of the street.*

*In 1933, deep into the Depression, there were five children in the family. (FF Collection)*

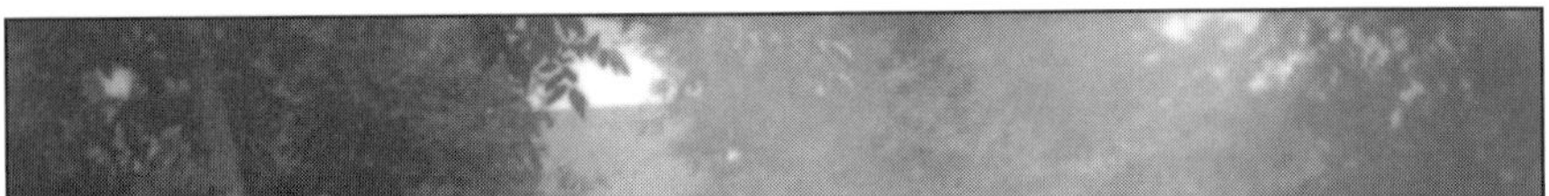

*In 1939, there were eight children in the family. (FF Collection)*

# 3
# The World is New

"Mother, Uncle Bill and Uncle Dean are here to help us move in," Dorothy said. "Can we go play now?" Two of Elmer's five brothers suddenly appeared at the back door. "We'll help move the heavy stuff into the house. Your husband doesn't look strong enough to lift a feather," Bill said as he pinched one of the kids standing by the door.

"Don't you worry, Bill, your brother can take care of himself when he needs to," Mother laughed. "Don't give him a hard time again today. There's too much to do, and you know how mad he gets when you kid him."

Bill's appearance always reminded me of a Walt Disney cartoon character that I had seen in one of his western classics. He wore a black ten-gallon hat that dwarfed him. Added to his half-shaven appearance was a homemade cigarette dangling from the side of his mouth. His small metal-rimmed glasses framed wide-open, innocent-looking eyes, masking his devilish plots. He was always thinking of a way to embarrass you until you almost cried. Especially the girls. His cowboy boots were worn outside of his Levi's that hung loose on his slight frame. All of his other brothers towered over him. Maybe that was the reason for his attitude of living: defense.

Uncle Bill was a rare breed of individual that comes along once in a blue moon. He had a unique outlook on life. His actions, his humor, his easy-going friendly spirit, all packed into a slight five-foot two or three inches, made him standout as a 'one-of-a-kind' person. His sense of humor bordered on genius. If he had had a Hollywood agent, he probably could have become the second Will Rogers of the Heartland. But then we could not have enjoyed his mischievous antics first hand, so it was just as well for us that he went undiscovered.

Bill was a garbage collector, or in modern phraseology, a sanitary engineer. He lived with his wife, Alt, and daughter, Opal, on the east edge of the city on Southeastern Avenue, not too far from the Cherry Rock Bridge and vegetable gardens. His partners were the Van Diepen boys from the Riverside area. They would start work early in the morning, four or five o'clock, driving their hard-rubber-tired Franklin truck to collect refuse from all over the city. Their route was made up of scattered households as the city had no organized garbage collection system. Hauling trash and garbage was left to free enterprise and the hustle of individuals such as Bill, much as they still do today. This was the type of job Bill liked and excelled at. He liked moving around the city, seeing people, and was at ease with all types of personalities.

Everyone liked Bill. You had to watch out, however, when he was around as he played tricks on you every chance he got. He especially liked to tease the kids. But he went about it in such a way that you knew he was only fooling. Even so, you didn't stand too close to him when you talked to him or ZAP—you got pinched on the leg, or the rear, or on the shoulder. The kids jumped a foot off the ground and yelped, but they loved it and always went back for more. His wife, Alt, was as gentle as Bill was rowdy, and she would caution him not to go too far with his tricks.

One day Bill got the brainy idea that he'd make his own wine. After getting the mixings, he put them in a crock in the barn to wait for nature to finish the job. A week later, after an especially warm stint of weather, his hired hand came running to the house to tell Bill that all hell had broken loose in the barn. Running to the barn they saw liquid running out from the bottom of the barn door. Cautiously opening the doors, they discovered that all of the bottles had exploded as the gases had tried to escape the capped bottles that he shouldn't have capped in the first place. He had not left room for the wine to ferment and they turned into vino-bombs.

................................

"Well, we'll get busy then, and leave the play until later."

The furniture was carried into the house and the beds were set up immediately. Boxes of canned goods were carried into the kitchen, along with the flour, sugar, coffee, and a box of freshly baked bread. Pots and pans were stored in the stove's oven.

The kids had been busy looking over the back yard. Norman suddenly ran inside and yelled "Mommy, what is this?"

"What is what?" she asked as she looked up from unpacking.

"Come look out the back window. I'll show you. Look down there, that thing by the porch."

"Oh, that, that's a cistern."

"A cis...cistern. What's that door go to?" he asked perplexed.

"That not a door, that's its cover to keep you from falling in. A cistern is used to collect the rain-water when it rains. We can use the water to wash the clothes, our hair, or take a bath in. We'll have to find out if it can still be used. Leave it alone. Don't take the top off, never take the top off, or you might fall into the water. Do you hear me?"

"Yes, Mom."

A cistern was a very important addition to the early prairie homes, be they in the city or the country. Until city water was available, the main source of water was by using a hand-pump from a well in the back yard. The water that nature supplied in the form of rain or melted snow seemed like a big waste to those pioneers who had to pump the water from the ground. In less rainy periods the water table could drop below the level of the pump and if the well ran dry you didn't have water until the next rain. A cistern was a way of beating the odds on the prairie. It was a hedge against nature.

When it rained, water was collected from the eaves of the roof and stored in these eight to ten-foot deep cement-lined holes. This provided a ready source of soft water for washing clothes or people. For the family Saturday-night bath or Monday washing day, the water was recovered by dropping a bucket with a rope tied to the handle into the cistern hole and a full bucket of water was pulled out hand over hand. Large fifteen-gallon galvanized tubs on the stove were filled up and heated for the wash and bath water. Later, as the city developed and grew more prosperous, city water from wells supplied fresh clean water through pipes all year around and the cistern became less important until they were finally not built anymore on the house lots.

Moving in didn't take long and the kids went out to play as soon as they were no longer needed. They were anxious to find out what awaited them in their new world. There was an entire neighborhood to explore before they would feel comfortable and able to sleep that night... and new friends to meet. Would the "natives" be friendly? What new toys would they find to play with? Would they like us or would they turn out to be snobs? Would they be too young to play with? or too old? Would their parents give us cookies? All of these questions had to be answered and Norm and Dorothy, the oldest kids, set about to do this. June and Charles had to be content to look from the confines of the yard this first day as they were the youngest.

Across the street, to the north, stood a two-story white wooden house with some sheds behind it. The building stood in the middle

of the block and to the east of it was a large garden. To its west were houses but they were facing to the west apparently onto the street to the west—Seventh Street. Norman and Dorothy were standing on the front porch of the house and talking to some kids who looked like they lived there.

Suddenly from the east a Ford automobile appeared and stopped in front of the house. Two ladies, one large and the other considerably smaller got out and stood looking around. Finally they left the car and began moving toward the house.

All at once, Mother threw open the back door and shouted "Ruth....Velva...Well, it took you long enough to get here." She ran to them and hugged them. "Come in, come in and see my house."

"We've got some food," the heavy one said. "We'll look first, then we will eat. We knew you wouldn't have time to cook so we brought your first meal in your new home."

"Oh, you're right. I haven't had time to feed the kids. I've been so busy. We'll look first. Come, I'll show you the house. The men are in the garage discussing something. We have the house to ourselves."

A half-hour later the women came out and began taking containers of food into the house.

"Get up to the table, supper time." Ruby urged the children who were playing in the back yard. Elmer, call the kids." she commanded. There was no need for another announcement. They dropped their playthings and came running.

..............................

Just as the pioneers had found less than a century before the Fredricks family set up house on Eighth Avenue, the land could be friendly during the warm months of the year. The cold winters could be brutal, however, unless one planned carefully for them.

Even then, survival was not ensured.

The kids playing across the street came quickly and as they approached the back door, Dorothy looked puzzled.

"Hey, Mom, what is this door back here?" Dorothy asked as she pointed to a door laying almost completely on its side.

"That's our cellar. Don't go down there. Stay away from it for now."

To the north of the back door was an entrance to the cellar. It wasn't a basement, it was a cellar. It appears that the person who decided to build a basement had second thoughts after starting to dig it. The excavation for the cellar ended half way under the house, and it was never finished off with a floor or sides. It was always cool and dark here under the house and this was where the potatoes from the garden as well as other vegetables were kept. In addition, a gas meter had been placed here: a gas meter that needed quarters inserted into it in order to get a specified amount of gas for cooking. A gas stove used for some of the cooking was in the makeshift kitchen, along with the wood-burning cook stove. Pandemonium sometimes broke out when the evening meal was being prepared and the flame of the stove began getting lower and lower. The allowance of the natural gas was running out. "Quick—find a quarter in my purse. Run to the cellar and feed the meter. Quick, before the fire goes out."

Two large rectangular wooden doors, when closed, kept the kids and animals out of the cellar. But you couldn't keep the kids off the cellar door. The large flat surface was too enticing to the children. Cellar doors were a common thing around most houses and it was used as a slide by the kids when the parents weren't looking. Their joy in sliding down them inspired a song of the '30's about rain barrels and cellar doors.

*Playmate, come out and play with me............*

*'Dressing up' to go to a movie in the 30's. (FF Collection)*

*On Sunday my brother, Norman, delivered newspapers and afterwards the family went to church. (FF Collection)*

# 4

# The Garden, Food and Things

In order to help keep the food bill down, our family planted a garden to the south of our house on Eighth. There bushels of potatoes were grown, as well as carrots, corn, and other vegetables. If I got hungry and needed a snack, all I had to do was go to the garden, pull up a carrot, clean it off, and begin eating. Tomatoes too were good fresh out of the garden.

Every spring a man would come around and ask Dad and others in the community if they wanted their gardens plowed. When he had enough lots to plow, he would come and do them.

All of the families around us had gardens. Dad worked at every opportunity in the garden when he was home in the evenings or on Sunday, the only day he had off from work at the Paint and Glass Company. It was a never-ending job to hoe and weed the garden. It was hot, back-breaking work. As kids we never fully appreciated this continual need to weed, and we shied away from doing these chores. Many a day the shovel and hoe remained leaning against the shed until our father came home and reminded us of our duty.

The first few months went well for the family on Eighth Avenue as they continued to settle into a new routine. It was a hot, sticky summer, but it wouldn't last forever. The cool nights of September would be a welcome relief.

Along with the shortening days of fall came the duty of returning to school. Dorothy, the oldest girl, now eight years old, entered the third grade. The oldest boy, Norman, began to attend for the first time.

A new school, a new set of friends. Norman wasn't shy, and he learned rapidly to take care of himself. The East Side kids played rough, and you had to learn to watch out for older kids and any bullies that were around. Routine 'kids' stuff' for the neighborhoods he had lived in. New kids were always given the 'treatment' at first to see if they fit in. Norman fit in, and he was good at making friends. Everyone respected his ability to take care of himself and they learned to leave him alone when he was mad. He had a temper! Nobody dared try to back him down if he was in the right. Taking care of yourself in Galesburg had to be demonstrated fast if you were to survive.

As we younger children watched with awe and curiosity, Dorothy and Norm left the house each morning and trudged away to we-knew-not-where. We could follow them for a block until the curb at Seventh and Seventeenth Street was reached. Here we dared not cross the street. There we stood and watched them go north to Beadle Elementary School and disappear from our small world.

The school was only six blocks from our home. It was a short walk to Fourteenth Street and Seventh Avenue, which took the kids very little time when they didn't play around on the way. Here they developed a new set of friends—Harvey, Skadson, Vosika, Monger, Halbritter, Slocum, Stearns, Engles, Eide, and many more. The area around Beadle school was very developed with houses and a grocery store was across from the school on Fourteenth Street. In anticipation of a land-buying and home-building boom in the Beadle School area, a trolley line had been built to connect with the downtown businesses. Things didn't materialize as anticipated and it went bankrupt. The tracks were pulled up.

..............................

As we quickly found out, there were many things to do in this new neighborhood. You could 'run' the neighborhood with the neighbor boys or prowl alone. There was always someone to go see or something to do at another kid's house. Anything to stay away from the house and the weeds in the garden. Because the area was not heavily developed with houses, the mothers could see almost the entire neighborhood area and keep their eyes on all that was happening to the kids. If we got into mischief, Mother heard about it from the neighbor mothers, and it never happened again, you could be sure of that.

If we got up early enough in the morning, we could claim the one bicycle the family owned. Whoever got it first in the morning could dictate the terms of riding it. However, if our bigger brother got it first, he would take off and we would not see him the rest of the day. Bummer. We younger kids had to stay closer to home. We couldn't go more than two blocks away from the house in either direction on Seventeenth Street or Eighth Avenue. If you rode north on Eighth the road dead-ended a block away and you had to turn around and ride back home or continue on Eighth to the tracks south of the house. It was a great enough distance for the smaller kids. After one trip we would have to trade off and let another ride it as we watched his progress on the same route. Unfortunately, broken chains or flat tires kept the second-hand bike inoperable much of the time.

The neighborhood around Seventeenth Street and Eighth Avenue was a kid's paradise to play in. There were great open spaces everywhere. To the east lived the Gartner family in their white, two-story house. This was the biggest, neatest house around. To the east of their house was the biggest temptation that could be offered to any boy—the Great Northern Railroad tracks. These tracks had been built for the north-south main line of the

Great Northern. In addition to these tracks there were a number of siding tracks. These were used for the switching of boxcars and temporary storage while they were being formed into larger trains for distant destinations. All this activity along the tracks fascinated me. The steam trains were most impressive and mysterious. Where did they came from and where were they were going? The steam that occasionally sprayed out of the engine was awesome. You kept your distance. It always seemed that the engineer knew our whereabouts and if we ventured too close, a flume of steam would come hissing out at us. We could see the engineer roar with laughter. He knew he had scared the hell out of us.

At times there would be no cars on the tracks and the area seemed lonesome. When only one or two boxcars were sitting on the tracks, it stimulated our interest, but when dozens would suddenly appear, it was playtime.

With help from a buddy, we could climb into the boxcars when the doors were open. This was very hard to accomplish until we were bigger and could jump higher. However, there were easier ways to do things. The metal ladders on each end of the boxcars were an open invitation. With a hand gripped for support as high as could be reached on the metal ladder, your leg could be put up on the lower bar of the ladder and with a grunt you could get on the ladder. Like monkeys, we would climb to the top of the boxcar using the metal ladders. Getting up was not our only peril. You had to keep an eye out for a train that might sneak up on you and connect to the cars. If that happened, you could get knocked off and fall ten or twelve feet to the ground below. When you were on the top of the boxcars, you could, with practice, avoid this by walking with a 'spread leg' position that gave support in case the car jerked. If the cars were refrigerator cars, the doors on top where the ice was stored could be opened and checked out. These open holes were cold and deep and this always scared me to death.

"Bet you're too scared to climb down into the ice container," was the usual taunt. I knew that if I fell in, I would never get out. "Nobody would find me ever," I said to myself, "and I would probably die." Life on the edge was exhilarating. The older boys had enough strength and height to get out of the holes when they went into them. The smaller kids needed help. Living on the edge of 'harms way' was the only way to go when you were a boy.

"Okay, I did it, now let's see you climb down in there, you chicken."

The steam engines ran on coal, and the coal sometimes fell out of the storage bin onto the rail tracks below. At times it would be collected by local families and used in the home stoves. This was a good way to cut down on the fuel bills. Lumber would sometimes be left in the boxcars and this was scavenged and taken home also.

..............................

Lawns were not a high priority in our world. However, our house was surrounded by what looked like a lawn. On closer inspection, the lawn was in reality a mat of green weeds that grew without watering and pretty much took care of itself. Money to keep a lawn vibrant, green, and groomed was better spent on food for the family.

Johnny Appleseed was a much respected legend by our family. We had two apple trees in the "lawn" area: one was a crab-apple tree on the north side of the house and another of forgotten variety was on the south-east side. Their beautiful white flowers in the spring gave us much pleasure but we could hardly wait until the little round fruit would be ready for eating. Watch out for the green apples though, they gave stomachaches if too many were eaten. The apples supplied the family with fresh fruit when they were ripe or they could be made into jam or jelly. However, two trees were not enough for our size family, so to supplement them, we sometimes took a Saturday or Sunday drive into the countryside. Whenever a berry bush was sighted along the road, the car stopped and we got out and picked berries until all of the pails were filled, or we got hungry and returned home.

The problem of too little space in the house plagued the family constantly, especially at night when everyone was home. Usually the children were too worn out from the day's play to bug the parents too much before going to bed. During the day the kids played outside and essentially the only person in the house was our mother. Food was often eaten outside under a tree. Get-togethers or birthday parties were held outside when the weather was good, but get-togethers in winter time had to be held at our Grandma Lane's house on the East side because her house was larger. Grandma Fredricks' house was also used for large get-togethers.

Today my family would be classified as an economically disadvantaged family and the public authorities would fall over themselves in the rush to offer us public assistance, but in the 1930s the majority of families survived and thrived under these seemingly adverse conditions. The family unit of the '30s was strong and produced very resilient children. In time of stress and need, the family retained its vigor with friends, neighbors and relatives helping out, even though they too might have had a large family to take care. We didn't feel underprivileged.

................................

The priorities of my father boiled down to providing rent for the house, food for the table, clothes for the kids, a car for him, and lastly, a movie occasionally for my mother.

Now that Dad had a steady job at the glass company, he was able to splurge and go to a movie with Mom on Wednesday nights. It was bingo night at the movies, and there was a chance of winning a plate or some other dish at the drawing the theater held. They could justify their night out by winning something for the home.

After a movie at the Orpheum on Wednesday's bingo night, Mom and Dad would stop by the Hamburger Inn to get a malted milkshake for Mom and burgers for both. The chance to sit down and enjoy a meal without being besieged by us kids must have felt heavenly. The fifteen-cent malt and the ten-cent hamburger of the '20s and '30s are long-gone, but the special feeling for the Hamburger Inn goes on.The Hamburger Inn was, to us, a city landmark in the 1930s. To the workers like my Father who seldom had the money to 'eat out', this place afforded the opportunity to give Mom a rare change from cooking at home. They felt comfortable here. No pretensions. The ten-cent hamburgers might have been a little thin meat-wise, but they were good and tasty, and people could afford them.

The money Dad made at his job did not allow enough for planning for the future or starting a savings account in a bank. Bank? He never had anything to do with a bank. He didn't borrow money for he didn't feel he could afford to pay somebody else, especially a bank, interest that he needed to buy food with. It was either cash or nothing. At least that's what he felt. The loan from the grocery store was okay because the store owner knew he was good for it at the end of the week. He always knew he needed to pay those small loans back first because he didn't want to anger the owner. Dad might need another loan when money got a little short again next week.

..............................

The kitchen was to the rear of the house and it had a cast-iron cook stove in it that was used for cooking and heating. It used wood and corn cobs for its fuel. The corn-cobs were gotten from a farmer friend. Behind this stove was a space large enough for us kids to crawl behind and get warm on cold mornings. All of the kitchen activity centered around this stove, especially on Mondays. Monday was always fondly remembered as 'bean' day. It was the day that Mom washed the clothes.

As there was no water heater in the house, the water had to be heated on the large iron cook stove. Early in the morning Dad had to get up and start a fire in the stove. Next he filled the large 15-gallon copper water tank on one side of the stove and any other containers he had. A breakfast of oatmeal was made for the family and the fire stoked continually to produce adequate heat for the large water containers. As the water was heating up, the washing machine was rolled into the kitchen and placed next to the stove. The room was getting crowded, even more as when the two galvinazed rinse tubs were brought in. After the water got hot enough, it was bucketed into

*Getting ready for a day of play in the backyard. (FF Collection)*

the washing machine, and then the washing could began. The containers on the stove were refilled and the water heated for the rinse tubs. By the time the first load of clothes was washed, the water was hot and this was then bucketed into the rinse tubs. The washing machine had a spring wringer on it that was used to wring out as much of the wash water as possible before the clothes were put into one of the rinse tubs. After sloshing the clothes around in the first rinse tub, the wringer was swung around and positioned toward the second rinse tub. The clothes were again wrung out by the electric wringer and sloshed around again and then wrung out again. This time the clothes were put into a wicker basket. When the basket was full, the laundry was taken out back and hung onto the metal clothes lines that ran from the house to the back shed. The three clothes lines were first wiped off the entire length of them with a damp cloth so the clothes would not get dirty. If it was winter, the clothes would freeze on the lines and when they were carried into the house they had to be set all over the house until they dried. The pungent wet odor of drying clothes permeated the entire house for hours.

This entire procedure of washing clothes for the large family would occupy my mother for the entire day from sun up to sun down. However, meals had to be prepared during wash time also. In order to feed the family, Mom had a system worked out that satisfied every one in the family. In the morning she would put a large pot of water on the stove and fill it was beans.

Beans took a long time to cook, almost all day, and little time was needed to watch them. After the kids went to school, she then made up a batch of bread in a large pan. Once this was mixed, the bread took time to rise and she was free to hang clothes on the line outside. By five o'clock, dinner time, the bread would be baked, the beans would be done, and the clothes washed.

Monday wash day was a full day of work for my mother.

*Mairzy doats and dozy doats and little lambs eat ivy.........*

William Crampton • Bob Czermak • Margaret Hansen Dachtler • Dorothy Vern Gene David Paulette Ruby Landon Swensen Teresa David Stellingwerf Roxanne David Jacobsen Phillip Tammy Crystal Bartling Troy Deneice Keith Daggett • Katherine Steve Stephenie G.C. Dawn Peters • Ken Shirley Donald Debra Keith Daggett • David Lee Verne Paulette Smith Eric Amy Gayl Daggett • Ruby Landon Deana Swanson • Teresa David Tony Amber Sadie Allan Stellingwerf • Roxanne David Tammy Geneva Jacobsen • Phillip Tammy Jensen Brett Danny Daggett • Crystal Natalie Bartling • Troy Deneice DeMent Daggett • Gwen Dahl • Richard Dargen • Tom Darr • Ron Decker • Dave Daniel David Dwain Williard Dorothy Joanne Dedrick • Bob Eddie Anderson Marv Bernie Tungue Bud Sween Dave Dedrick • Jennie DePew • George Carolyn DeShazer • Beulah Engles Desautels • Bill Dickey • Lois Dixon • Buell Donaldson • Tom Donley • Gypsy Douglas • Bill Dougherty • Charlotte Kavenagh Dreyer • George Dunham • Jean Dunham • Ernie Ducky Bunnie DuPue • John Eich • Clara Eide • Don Ed Eide • Dal Doug John Egan • Ron Eggiman • Robert Eleeson • Paul Eldridge • Windy Elliott • Jim Bob Elmen • Carrol Engebretson • Lynn Engen • Jean Ruth Songstrad Beulah Desautels Dorothy Hansen Ellen Bagche Stephenson Dick Ray Engles • Dick Enright • Joyce Norman Sherron Norma Karen Floyd Ruth Enstrom • Fern Nessan Erickson • Dick Erickson • Charles Darrell Don Bill Erickson • Duff Erickson • Betty Erickson • Blanche Harvey Falor • Dale Fellows • James Fenner • Darwin Erwin Fields • Emery Fillmore • Duane Fines • John Fliginger • Henriette Rose Floren • Duane Myron Floren • Bernell Fonder • Clarence Lily Marlene Carolyn Ron Foss • Arlene Foster • Charles Lois William Eugene Frank George Elmer Della Etta Hazel Bernard Don Evelyn Brown Cullen Dean Lucille Evert Ruth Fredricks • Frank Velva Fredricks Grace Powderly Katherine Hiett Harold Jeanne Hudson Fredricks • William Penn Angeline Charles Ruby Elmer Norma Dorothy Norman Charles June Dick James Nancy Frank Fredricks • Elmer Agnes Freese Dorothy Daggett Norman Elaine June Harlen Dick Peggy Kim Karol James Nancy Reuter• Frank Kay Fredricks • Nancy LuAnn Ralph Art Reuter • Norman Elaine Klinghagen Nancy Carol Jo Bruce Fredricks • James Douglas Jeffery James Joseph Charles Fredricks • Frank Kathryn Nye Susan Steven Sherry Fredricks • Harold Iona Barnes Larry Lonnie Sandra Kathy Fredricks • Fred Fern Grindy Gary Freese • Art Agnes Fred Sonny Dorothy Irene Robert Barbara Bott Duane Fines David Roger Alyce Dale Holly Butler • George Alice Art Myrtle Irwin Helen Meek Mildred Jurgenson Lester Esther Mofle Freese • Bill Friedhoff • Dick Gage • Bob Garrett • Minnie Ester Bailey Mary Clark Roy Gaertner Gartner • Ole Garvick • Marlee Gefke • Darrell Gehzus • Charles Gerlinger • Floyd Gilbransons • Donald Ginther • Polly Girton • Gordon Graff • Don Grebin • Sherrill Greenlee •

*(continued on page 40)*

# 5
# Grocery Stores

While my family lived on the East Side for many years, they traded at the grocery store at the corner of Blauveldt and Seventh Street. This two-story brick rectangular store was run by two sisters and their brother who lived upstairs of the store.

These 'Mom and Pop" stores were not as flashy as the stores are nowadays. Many times they were built by the family that ran them. This store had two large plate glass windows by the front entrance facing Blauveldt. They never had displays of anything in them that I can remember and dead flies piled up on the inside ledge below the hanging sticky flypaper that lured the bugs to their doom. An occasional community notice was stuck in the corner of the window by the door and these lingered there long after the event was over.

Old loyalties and friendships were hard to give up in the early days. This was no exception with trading at a grocery store. Not all of the food that was needed could be grown in gardens. Pigs and chickens could no longer be raised within the city limits and fresh meat had to be bought from a store or a farmer friend. Coffee, flour, and increasing types of canned goods had become necessities and not just thought of as luxuries.

This was a down-to-earth type of store and one of the few buildings that our family went into and felt comfortable in. Neither banks nor fancy stores were ever frequented by my family as they never had the money to spend in them and it wasn't until I was over ten years old that I went to a restaurant of our neighbors and was given a meal of hamburger steak and French fries after working in the kitchen for two hours. I was amazed. I had never dreamed that there were businesses that actually cooked other people's food as I had always eaten at home. My world was greatly expanded in this one episode.

The selection of groceries by customers in the Depression of the '30s was not taken lightly, as every penny had to count. Items were looked over, discussed, considered and reconsidered until final selection occurred. Even then when the cost was totaled up, many items were put back on the shelf if they could be done without. Items not affordable but desired were many times felt, caressed, and then put back on the wooden shelves by my mother. Everywhere you walked in the store, the wooden floor would creak as you made your way across it to the center counter where the groceries were taken after selection. No shopping carts were available for the customers. The sisters would wait at the counter and talk to each other in voices too low to be heard except for a occasional word. If a price of a item was not written on it, you had to ask the clerks. After items were taken to the counter, they were written in a receipt book and totaled when the shopping was finished. These items were put in a cardboard box or wooden crate that were kept in the storeroom in the back of the store.

Anxious moments and sweaty palms were noticed when it came time to total up the food bill. If the two or three dollars worth of groceries were needed but my folks were short of money, one of the clerks would put the list and total amount owed into a ledger they kept below and behind the counter. This happened very often when overtime work was not being done by my father. The store owners understood this and everyone agreed that it would be paid as soon as money was available. When my dad paid his bill, the owner would always hand my father a cigar and some candy for the kids.

..............................

The move to Eighth Avenue in 1933 added a considerable distance to the trip to the familiar grocery store the family had shopped at on the East Side, but even so the family continued to shop for groceries at it. In addition they purchased items from a traveling salesman who worked for the Jewel Tea Company. This visit by the truck became an excited event for the kids. The odors that emanated from his goods were wonderful and the variety was something to marvel at.

However, other things were needed during the week from a real grocery store, so occasionally in the winter my oldest sister and brother would pull their sled with a wooden box tied on it to the East Side store for a order of groceries. After loading the sled with the groceries they would return to Eighth and Seventeenth Street by way of the Cliff Avenue bridge over the Sioux River. This was a long trip for such young kids but the family could not afford a second car for our mother to use to run errands.

Over the years, the population of Sioux Falls increased and a new type of grocery store developed. The newer stores were owned by companies or large groups of people and they were well-financed and well-stocked. The neighborhood 'mom and pop' grocery stores, by contrast, were owned by an individual and run by him and his wife and sometimes the children also. Service was extremely personal and they bent over backwards to help you. The family usually lived on the premises—upstairs or in the back room—where they could be found almost day and night. Their margin of profit was small and they survived only as long as the family ran them.

The new breed of grocery store was usually a 'chain' operation with paid professional management help and numerous clerks. In these clean, attractive stores the hours were fixed and the stores were well-stocked with an assortment of goods that went beyond the minimum needs of the customer.

They operated on a volume concept that produced a profit to the investors. Food was bought in bulk amounts and the savings were passed on to the customer.

This new type of approach was the death knoll to the 'mom and pop' stores. Competition was tough and few survived for very long. They survived until greater accessibility of the automobile occurred in the family. Most of these stores were only memories by the end of the 1940s.

The new stores like Sunshine, Economy, Pigglie-Wigglie, and Red Owl cropped up everywhere in larger and newer building in the downtown area. After a move to Third Avenue by our family, the ties were severed with the Seventh and Blauveldt Grocery Store and our family succumbed to the supermarkets like almost everyone else. This event went unnoticed in the newspaper of the Argus Leader because it was a subtle shift in the community values. Subtle shifts of community changes are seldom noticed by newspapers and many historians can only by hind-sight interpret the importance of these changes in American culture. But a change in the culture was occurring with this mass market concept that was later carried over into all phases of our society.

Competition eventually drove Loomis, Hiatt, and Edmonds Grocery stores out of business and the small corner family owned-and-run grocery store ceased to exist. They are now, after many years, being duplicated by the more sophisticated 'mom and pop' store at the service stations in the form of the 7-11 convenience stores.

..............................

For the house-bound mother in the Heartland, Saturday offered a change from the monotony of doing the dishes, making the beds, scrubbing the linoleum floors, washing clothes, and preparing meals. Although the work week for the male included Saturday until usually five o'clock, after work and dinner, my dad and mother would go to the grocery store shopping in the evening. This was occasion to dress up so my mother and father would put on their second-best-looking clothes for the trip downtown. Father would sometimes wear a suit for the occasion. All of the kids stayed at home with the oldest, Dorothy, taking care of the rest of the tribe. It gave a certain authority to the older sister when she was made the 'official' authority for the evening. The kids viewed her with a different type of respect as she was constantly telling them that if they didn't mind her she'd tell Dad. She liked the status and at the same time she hated to do it. It would be great, she thought, if she could do something for herself for once without the obligation of taking care of the kids. The responsibility was very heavy for her. "Stay out of the cupboards and behave," they were admonished by the parents as their car backed out the dirt makeshift driveway at the side of the house. As dad backed the Studebaker out he had to make sure the fire hydrant by the curb was not hit. Immediately after they left one or two of the younger kids would drift into the house and head for the kitchen with only one goal in mind. There they would open the doors of the cupboards and begin a systematic search for food of any sort that may have been hidden by our mother. Cookies, donuts, and graham crackers, anything to munch on, was their goal. A chair would be pulled to the cupboard and every shelf would be scrutinized. If Dorothy hadn't caught wind of what was going on in the house by the time the search was finished, Joe and Nancy could go out and play with a clear conscience that there was nothing in the house to eat.

..............................

The Sunshine Grocery Store on Twelfth and Second Avenue, across from the Post Office, was the most commonly patronized grocery store by my parents in the late '30s and the '40s. The Economy Grocery Store on the south side of the Post Office on Phillips was a second choice but many of their prices were a little higher than the Sunshine.

I vividly remembers the donut-making machine by the coffee counter in the front of the store by the Twelfth Street door exit. This was a fascinating bit of machinery. Donut dough was gently squeezed from a mechanism from a hopper in the top onto hot oil below it. The dough dropped between two small paddles that were attached to a center shaft that moved the paddles around in a circle. The dough was carried through the hot oil and they baked on one side in the oil. Half way around the circle path, a three pronged spatula turned the donuts over onto the uncooked side and as the donuts kept moving in the circle, they finished cooking until completely golden brown. Before reaching the starting point of the circle another spatula lifted the finished donut out of the oil and that space was ready for another shot of donut dough from above. Then the process was repeated. Again and again producing dozens of donuts. The hot donuts looked marvelous and if you had a nickel you could get a cup of coffee with two of these donuts. Most of the time this was a watching experience but in my mind was always the hope that the clerk or someone passing by would offer a donut to eat. The clerk did this with a quick wink of the eye most of the time as she hurried away to the far end of the counter. How could anyone resist doing this good deed for a tow-headed youngster standing in front of a donut machine?

If the grocery shopping session went fast, as it usually didn't, my father stayed in the store and looked around following mom and getting a few items for her. Usually he was only in the way. He would get bored and wander outside to talk with a group of regular shopping husbands that were bored also. Small talk about acquaintances in other jobs was bantered about, and what each one thought of another approach and attitude to work was discussed. This type of bull session actually accomplished a couple of important things for these men. Car parts were needed and repair done and if some piece of work around the house needed to be done, discussing it helped the men solve many problems that were important to them. It was an informal problem solving session and swapping information and techniques that kept the house and cars going at the lowest price possible. If no one knew how something was to be done, their pool of information would find it out. And if one needed help with some work, this barter system helped provide a solution. They were all in the same boat, life was expensive, money was scarce, and everyone at one time or another would need help. If you helped someone on a project, you weren't expected to accept money, but an implied future help was expected. This was how the working community in the City rolled smoothly.

Events of the area were related and by the time the shopping session was over, the men knew about what had happened in and around the area. Most didn't get the Argus Leader newspaper and this was the community newspaper for the shoppers.

*Oh what a beautiful morning, oh what a beautiful day..........*

# 6
# Dad's Job

In the beginning of the 1930s everyone was in the same sinking boat.

Everybody had just enough to get by on and conditions were not enough to incite rebellion by those out of work, but it was rough going making a living. The hope of getting a job consumed my father. He wanted the same economic benefits that a few others enjoyed. People still had cars although they did not have work. People were still able to pay rents although some months it was slim goings. Time grew heavy on many people that normally had jobs and they felt bad that they couldn't provide money for the family.

Vegetable gardens were relied upon more than ever for basic food and 'going out' was not in many families' vocabularies. Simple pleasures like conversations, playing cards with neighbors and friends, and working in gardens were thought of as well-accepted pursuits. An occasional five-cent movie was something that lasted in the memory for weeks after it was over.

Money was tight. You hoped that enough money would be available to buy the basics for the table. And maybe enough for a car. The house could suffer, curtains could be made, wash towels could be made out of flour sacks and clothes were handed down to the younger kids until they wore out. Everything was recycled and recycled until every ounce of good was drawn out. Nothing was wasted.

For my father, the '20s was one of drifting from one job to another. He had married my mother in 1922 and they lived in separate households until the first child was due—a year and a half after marriage. During this time, he shoveled coal for the Parmley Coal Yard when work was available. His formal education ended at the fifth grade level when the family moved to here from Ponka, Nebraska. The change of cities seemed like a good time to make the break from his schooling. He never returned after moving onto a farm south of town. He knew that jobs could be had without education—there would always be a need for ditch diggers, farm labor, collecting garbage, draying—they would always be needed. His family had gotten along without having permanent employment and they had survived O.K. It would work for him, too. Unfortunately this type of thinking halted his rise in jobs the rest of his life, and he knew it. That is possibly why he encouraged me in subtle unspoken ways to continue staying in school as long as I could. I ended up being the second in the family to finish high school and the first in the family to start and finish college.

A family was expected after marriage occurred. You took what you got. There was no talk of abortions or vasectomies and for that matter, sex was not discussed by either partner. Everything was learned 'firsthand' with on-the-job training the only lesson.

Any sex discussed was in the pulp magazines and this sex was of the "kinky", perverse kind that left a repulsive stigma about much intimacy. The Bible didn't approve of this approach to sex. The pulp magazine clandestine back-room operations of abortions left grave lessons to young boys for sex out of marriage. Without any preventative approach of pregnancy, the young married male and female could only hope that God would be only a little generous in his granting of fertility in the family. In our family he was overly generous.

The first child of Elmer and Ruby died after having only three days of existence, and the second child, Dorothy, was born over a year later. The third child, Norm, was born in 1928. In 1930 another boy, Charles, was born. It was becoming clear that some permanent job had to be found as he could not rely on temporary employment. It was getting harder to keep even with the bills.

A friend of Dads, Ernie, had gotten a job at the old livery building that now housed the Paint and Glass Company at the foot of Ninth Street by the river and he suggested to Elmer that he should try to get one there too. Elmer was a good, eager, willing helper and the men around him knew he was reliable. There was no need to stand over him to see that a job would be done properly, he was very self-reliant and trustworthy.

The Paint and Glass company had a receiving dock on the east side next to a spur line for the Rock Island railroad where the freight cars were unloaded. Extra help was sometimes needed to get the job done fast if a lot of orders were pending due to a tornado or a wind storm. When a storm hit the area, glass was the first thing to be broken. Sometimes entire towns would have every glass broken in a windstorm and a crew from the Paint and Glass might spend an entire month putting in glass due to nature's rampage. If you were available at the right time, work was available.

Elmer had been told, 'be available' by the foreman. As he had not been working for a period of time, he had developed the habit of being at the dock in the morning as the men arrived at work. He was a well-liked individual that could talk to anyone.

As the end of another week approached early in 1932, renewed hope for a job was awakened in him as a train started crossing the Sioux River railroad bridge just to the north of the Paint and Glass. Ever alert of the happenings around the dock, he knew that this train had to be coming to the dock and that this was going to be his lucky day. Many trains had been crossing the trestle this week but his intuition told him that this was for the Paint and Glass. The train slowly moved past the tracks that were about 40 feet to the east and parallel to the dock, but it had to maneuver for over two blocks to get onto this siding. The train slowly went past the building, crossed the Tenth Street highway a block away and passed out of sight on the curve past the Rock Island depot. Elmer kept watching in the direction of the train in anticipation of its return on this side-track. Finally this waiting was rewarded and the back of the cars could be seen as the train slowly backed toward the dock. Slowly.... Slowly... Now all of his attention was on the event of the train on the siding. Workers from inside the shop had drifted out from behind the large wooden doors that led into the shop. With hands thrust into their bib overalls and a idle curiosity of the situation, they joked with each other and watched the train back closer. John, the foreman, eventually came out, creating a momentary uneasiness in the workers until they felt it was okay to watch. After a few minutes, John spun around and hurriedly went into the shop only to return a few seconds later with some large papers in his hand. Glancing at the boxcars and then back at the papers a few times, he turned around and looked at Elmer. 'You want a job?' Dad leaped forward and opened his mouth to say 'yes' but it didn't come out easily. John looked down at the papers again and passed one to Ernie and told him to have Elmer help him get the freight checked out and unloaded as soon as he could.

A job! He knew it was his lucky day.

This afternoon job turned out to be the beginning of a permanent job that lasted for thirty five years at the Paint and Glass. The pay was $25 a week at first but as the recession grew worse, the pay was reduced to $15 per week until the end of the 1930s.

..............................

As growing youngsters, we were always hungry and ready to eat anything. But the biggest treat was a hamburger on a bun and a 'long john' sweet roll to follow it down. Either one would be gladly devoured and to get both was like a round trip to heaven.

The working men of Sioux Falls were accustomed to taking a coffee break around 10:00 AM and I knew this. It was, therefore, no accident that I often showed up at my Dad's shop at coffee-break time. As the break time approached, the men of the Sioux Falls Paint and Glass would begin to look at their pocket watches, laying them in the palms of their hands to examine them as if they weren't working quite right. There was almost no project that couldn't be laid aside and attended to after the break. When the break time came, they would drift to the large doors at the rear of the building that led into the alley behind, and they would start the daily walk to their favorite coffee spot. The Nickel Plate on Phillips Avenue by the E.C. Olson store was closer to the back door, but this was a classier coffee spot than they wanted. The bright chrome stools and tables of the Nickel Plate made them feel less comfortable in their soiled overalls.

The preferred spot was at a well-known established institution in town called the Hamburger Inn. This 12 by 20 bunker-type block building sat next to the alley on Tenth Street. A large window in the front allowed the proprietors, Stan and his partner, to keep tabs on the movements of cars up the highway and watch for customers. A friendly hand wave was returned by anyone who walked in front of the window. In turn, the cooks could be seen all during the day flipping over the small hamburger patties on the grill by the window. They did a brisk business of selling the best 10-cent burgers in town.

If you were lucky enough to get one of the twelve seats in the always-busy Inn, you had a small section of counter in front of you to put your coffee and hamburgers on. If you got there anywhere around ten o'clock, I just resigned myself to the fact that I had to stand while enjoying coffee and donuts or a hamburger. You knew you were lucky to even get into the cafe at this hectic time. The constant jostling of customers getting up and moving out through this mass of humanity made it quite an achievement not to spill your coffee.

'Stan, coffee over here... and that roll over there. No, black! How much? You sure? What'd you do, raise your prices? O.K., here you go. On the counter.'

After the ten o'clock rush eased off, the Big Three Garage mechanics from across the alley would mosey on over for their coffee. Burt would sometimes go with them if he was around and not off attending to the city's business.

Stan knew the routine of all of his customers, as he had been doing business with them for many, many years. Dusty from the Weatherwax Clothing store never sat down for his coffee. As soon as Stan saw him crossing the street, he poured his coffee and set it on the counter. After pouring in a slug of cream and stirring in two spoons of sugar, it was cool enough to drink down quickly, and out the door he went again—waving his hand as he went across the Tenth Street traffic. Everyone knew Dusty would bet on anything. He'd lost two fortunes gambling. He would bet on which of two raindrops running down a pane of glass would arrive first, and he usually lost.

...............................

I liked to visit with the good-natured and friendly men that my dad worked with. Their work of cutting and setting glass, polishing the edges at a large belted emery wheel and occasionally building and packing crates of glass for shipping out of town were exciting activities to watch.

The front office was a part of the business that was sort of forbidden for us to explore. And quite naturally that mystique intrigued me. It fascinated me beyond understanding. That was where the salesmen worked and paint, wallpaper, and glass were ordered and sold. The orders for Dad's work came from out of the front office. The men in the front office had high school and college educations and they were the first achievers in the business world that I had contact with. I looked upon them with awe. What they did to achieve such a high status among the people I knew intrigued me. They lived a different standard from that of the families I knew and they dressed in suits every day, not only on special occasions. The women clerks and secretaries were different in many ways from my cousins and sisters. I liked the way the people in the front office conducted themselves. There was no social contact with them except at the office although I was familiar with the section of town where they lived. They had newer cars, better homes, clothes, and a social status that I hoped someday I would achieve, if ever I could figure out how to get it.

That these thoughts and impressions were going on in my head as I looked at these white-collar men and women was something they never knew. However their lives greatly influenced me, although they probably never knew it, as I spoke very little to them as I passed through their office to the workshop in the back of the building where my father worked.

## *JACK ARMSTRONG—THE ALL-AMERICAN BOY*

Ron Greenslate • Dick Bonnie Kari Lisa Gregerson • Lenita Prouty Groos • Hiram Calla Mae Yaeger Richard Janie Cloud Grow Georgia Gulbrandson • Everett Gulbrandson • Dick Guenther • Sally Haas Mrs Haas • Millce Hackett • Carolyn Haga • Kenny Wes Halbritter • Shirlee Hammarley • Barbara Dick Hanger • Gary Sandra Kathy Jo Hanson • Dorothy Engles Hansen • Elinor Hanson Hansen • Babe Stearns Hanson • Lois Becker Hanson • Pauline Hanson • Thomas Hanson • Dick Harriman • Ted Harriman • Marilyn Caldwell Harmer • Gary Hartenhoff • Lee Bob Blance Falor Evelyn Pelley Harvey • Ken Hasting • Harriet Hegstrum Hauge • Marian Slaman Haugstad • Veloy Hawkey • Lorraine Conklin Hayes • Sybil Conklin Hayes • Julie Hegstrum • Luella Hegstrum • Elaine Heiser • Kayle Helgerson • Dwane Hennings • Don Hewitt • Charles Hibbison • Jim Higgens • Edith Hill • Yvonne Joan Val Rae Hill • Connie Hines • Chuck Norm Hines • Shirley Maggie Ethyl Hodges • Darlene Buckley Betty Twedt Hoefert • Charlynn Hoefert • Jack Hoffman • Roger Hoier • Marilyn Holly • Dwight Hoover • Dave Hopewell • Merle Horton • Robert Houck • Geneva Houg • Ruth Billie Howalt • Jim Chuck Howlin • Chad Hoyme • Jeanne Granville Dorothy Marjorie Linda Brenda Hudson • Henry Russell Robert Janet Huhn • Arthur Huseboe • Dean Hutton • L. Joy Ingalls • Diana Basil Irish • Dick Irvine • Cecil Myrtle Freese Loren Dolly Irwin • Monte Irwin • Don Irwin • Bently Jaco • Ron Jamtgaard • Betty Rahn Jasper • Joanna Caldwell Jocelyn • Carole Johlfs • Jim Johnson • Pat Johnson • Ron Johnson • Martha Johnston • Minnie Bill Merlyn Dorothy Bob Swavely Carol Ken Peggy Fredricks Jones • Carol Wyman Kent Hoover • Kenneth Juanita William John Katherine Jones • Stanley Bob Roy Jones • Joanne Jones • Barrett Jones • Jerry Jonke • Julie Letner Jordan • Donald Jorgensen • Roy Jurgensen • Joan Peachy Gilbrandson Jorgenson • Leona Kearney • Jan Keenan • Dick Kelley • Myron Kelley • Charles Kemerling • James Kepford • Maxine Killeaney • Dona Kirkeby • Harold Kirkegaard • Marilyn Kirkpatrick • Jim Kirschman • Bob Kirschman • Joe Klock • Andrew Kleinsasser • Jim Kolb • Paul Betty Ball Kolb • Evelyn Sorgdrager Kraft • Bill Kraft • Dick Kraft • Don Krenos • Addie Larson Keep Krogmann • Wally Krohn • Bob Krueger • Lv Kruger • Avis Calkins Kruse • Lee LaFollett • Bob Lamb • John Carrie Doris Chambers Geneva Johnson Roy Russell Ruby Fredricks Carrie Carlson Lawrence Gerald Vance Joyce Enstrom Lane • Lawrence Serena Jane Heither Janet Lee Lane • Bob Larson • Bill Larson • Frankie Larson • Dwane Leach • Lee Avis Kruse Delores Parker Joan Pedersen June Ranney Lehman • Lorelei Letner • Gussie Adams Lewis • Duane Lewis • Walter Leyse • Frances Line • Joanne Livingston • Arlene J. Hoefert Lofswold • Bill Lowe • Dick Lueders • Florence Lyng • Joan Mabee • Gladys Machmiller • Bernice Rose Mager • Kenny Malloy • Norma Tyler Main • Dean Mann • Bill Bob Mannion • Shirley *(continued on page 86)*

# 7
# Picnics

"Elmer, let's have a picnic this weekend." Ruby said as she walked out to the hard-tried truck that dad had driven home in. He could 'borrow' the truck to get home in after work, the boss didn't mind, especially if he had worked extra time.

"Picnic? This weekend? Okay. Sounds like fun."

So it was settled. They would have a picnic.

In the 20s and 30s family picnics in the Heartland were events that produced fond memories that persisted for years to come. They were fun where everyone experienced good fellowship, excellent food, renewal of family ties, an exciting time, and a time for catching up on the affairs of the family.

Grandmothers, grandfathers, mothers, fathers, cousins, and distant relatives were always welcome.

Everyone looked forward to them. Preparation by the kids was negligible but to ensure success there were many days of preparation needed by the women of the families. This they did with gusto. If there were no watermelons in their garden they had to be bought at the store or gotten from a neighbor in exchange for some other type of vegetable. Potatoes had to be dug out of the garden, or brought up from the cellar, and peeled to make a mountain of potato salad. The pantry had to be inventoried to ensure that there was enough kool-aid and jello mix available along with a couple of cans of mixed fruit for the jello. Fresh homemade bread and rolls had to be baked. A million and one details that only a mother knew had to be sorted out.

This was an occasion when paper plates were used. The fewer the dishes that needed to be washed, the better. All of the metal spoons, knifes, forks, and paper cups had to be taken along as plastic utensils had not been invented at this time. Lemonade and red colored kool-aid that left a red mustache when you drank it was put in gallon Thermos jugs to take along. Two or three jugs were needed and more would be made up at the picnic. The large metal gallon coffee pot was taken along. This was the first item that was placed on the iron grates of the fireplace when we arrived at the Elmwood Park picnic grounds in West Sioux.

The rural community of West Sioux seemed like another town to us. And it was. Way to the west of town, although it was incorporated into Sioux Falls, the mile plus of open spaces between the end of Sixth Street and the Brockhouse Grocery Store isolated it from the City proper. The nature of these fiercely independent West Sioux citizens dictated that they wanted to be thought of as a separate town. The West Sioux park area had developed as a pleasure center early in the history of development of Sioux Falls. It had been a natural spot for picnics and outings for years. The muddy brown-colored Sioux River water with its muddy banks slowly snaked and meandered through the acres of grounds to the northwest of Sioux Falls and it had provided an opportunity for relief by swimmers in the hot, humid afternoons. Paddle boats could be rented for trips on the river, a dance hall had been built for the pleasure of the adult crowd that sought romance and a good time. It was a good place to meet potential mates. Many a future husband and wife met on the dance pavilion floor, dancing to the music of Lawrence Welk.

As weekends or holidays neared, the weeds were cut down with a horse-pulled mower in anticipation of the many city folk that were to visit the area. A softball game could be played almost anywhere it was level. All you needed was a few willing players and a softball. However, the kids weren't interested in the adult games of softball or horseshoes. After an uncomfortable time spent getting over their initial shyness, they wanted to play and the wide open spaces were perfect for them. They made up their games as they saw fit—kick the can, hide and seek, freeze, pump-pump-pull away, and many other that only they understood. One activity that always seemed to be fun was chasing each other. For what reason? Who knows. One minute two kids would be talking, and the next minute there was a chase and catch game. Their life wasn't complicated yet. They didn't need reasons for their activities. They knew the reason. Just figuring out who your cousins were was a tough enough task. There were no doors to open or remember not to slam on the way out, they could run around yelling without worrying about being too loud. Adults and parents were to be avoided for most of the day and that suited both sides just fine. It was hard to get into trouble on a picnic unless you hit or bossed someone too much. The only admonishments we received was when we got too close to the tables with the food waiting on them. 'Don't get into the food yet.' were the most dreaded words you could hear on a picnic. It was hard to stay away as the food piled up on the tables as the noontime grew nearer. The stomachs growled and the bodies automatically knew it was getting near to feast time.

As we edged our way toward the food tables, we anxiously waited for everything to get ready.

The table full of food and pungent with odors was almost too much for a kid to stand. Hot dogs were being boiled. Coffee was brewed and ready for the cups. The bread was being sliced and the hamburgers were being fried. Finally it was ready. Grab a paper plate and get a spoon and a knife. Potato salad was heaped upon the plate, alongside the jello and beans. The bread with the hamburger was set upon this and a cup of lemonade or kool-aid was juggled in one hand while the paper plate with the food was in the other.

*In 1937, west Sioux Falls was a 'quaint' town on the way to the Elmwood Park. (The West Sioux Story—C. Smith)*

*A picnic was a time for good food and family pictures in West Sioux. (FF Collection)*

This had to be a careful balancing act to avoid bumping anything or anyone. Finally and almost none too soon, a spot at a bench or on the ground was found and the food began disappearing down the mouth. The hunger and feeding frenzy of a child at a picnic can be appreciated and understood only as it is happening. Afterwards neither can be fully described. What a sensation while it is happening. What contentment.

What a life! It can't get any better than this. The same food at home never had a taste like this. A second hot dog and a little more jello and a huge piece of chocolate cake would polish off a perfect meal. And then off again to play. No rest. The red mustache from the kool-aid disappears on the sleeve of the shirt as the parents yell to us to 'be careful'.

After the food on the tables are covered up, the pace of the day for the adults slows even more. The pleasurable conversations and company plus the large meal made everyone sleepy. One by one a favorite spot on a blanket beneath a tree is found and before long a 'big quiet' develops all around. Those who did not succumb to sleep have lowered their voices as the others drift off to sleep. The men worked hard during the week and this chance to snooze was a respected break of activity for them. After an hour or so the bodies began to stir again and low conversations began to occur again. Avoiding the bright sunlight, groups of women began discussing the babies' lives, their home problems in the kitchen, and family goings on. Gossip about what the younger members of the family were doing or whom they were seeing would bring feigned surprise by those who knew. From these 'sessions' everyone kept abreast of the happenings of the family.

The men finally succumbed to pranks of their sisters-in-law or brothers-in-law. A few would be good naturedly hung upside down by their legs and everyone got a big laugh out of it. The men's hats were put on girls and pictures taken. All had a good time at this. A softball game would be started. Suit coats would be taken off and laid aside and a good-natured game would begin. Strikes and balls were disputed by all and the final score of the game was never clear. This lasted until players got thirsty or hungry or both and everyone started drifting toward the tables of food. The meal was on again. What hadn't been eaten at noon was soon cleaned up as potato salad disappeared and any meat left was made into sandwiches. Coffee and cake finished off the second round of eating. The coffee drinking could linger on for hours if the weather was nice. If it was too hot, lemonade was the choice of drink.

Dishes, pots, pans, tablecloths, and all remaining dishes would slowly be accumulated on one table and put into boxes for the return trip home. This could take an hour or two, depending on the mood of everyone. Some days nobody felt like hurrying home if it was still too warm. No need to go home if it was still hot. If the weather had been cool or rain menacing, they moved briskly to avoid potential afternoon downpours. Most picnics were not ruined by rain, however. God wouldn't be that cruel.

*Slide down my cellar door................*
*And we'll be jolly friends for ever more.*

*In the '30s there was fun for all at the Elmwood Park picnic grounds in West Sioux. (FF Collection)*

# 8
# Church

Saturday morning: kids home from school, but other than that, almost the same routine as during the week.

Sunday morning: no going to work for Dad today. Day off. At least as far as going to his regular job was concerned. However, it was church time. Sleep later than usual. Take your time getting up. Eat a leisurely breakfast of pancakes, syrup, sausages, coffee, then wash up, put on your best clothes, pile into the truck and drive to church.

Although it has not always been appreciated by all parents, every little suggestion and voice tone are noticed by the developing child. Many thoughts and ideas would be better off not said or suggested to this bundle of reception. During this developing period, attitudes, morals, mores, conduct, and the outlook of life is greatly influenced. Spoken words become indelibly imprinted in the child's self-conscious mind. Make no mistake about it, a child begins learning immediately after birth.

The first five years of life are the most fertile learning period in a person's lifetime. The touching, feeling, hearing, smelling, and tasting senses are at work and receptive 24 hours of the day. A child learns his language and concepts of many vocabulary words in these first very fertile years. It would be great if one could continue learning at the rate that a person does in his first five years of life, but, unfortunately, we don't.

Many times this rate of learning is slowed down and inhibited by society and parents themselves. "Be quiet, don't make a fool of yourself," or "Leave that alone, don't get into trouble," imprints on our psyche that childhood exploration is not to be tolerated or accepted, thus cutting short our curiosity of much of the world around us.

In spite of these known facts, society has yet to awaken itself and take full advantage of the child's potential. It continues to be a mystery of paramount importance the way we still educate children. We leave it to the parents to make these decisions. For almost all children the first five years of life are lacking in any formalized professional approach that takes advantage of this receptiveness to learning... unless they are introduced to a church or religion.

Although these institutions of God in themselves profess goals different from surrounding churches, they lend a cohesion to the society that is remarkable in its similarity. They produce goals of confidence, education, and eternal hope in the society as well as religion, acceptance of one's state of being, pride in oneself, and self reliance—goals that allow a society to function on a civilized level. Not every one of these concepts is produced equally well in every church of the Midwest, but over all they have become the character to achieve by the Midwesterners.

For the immature, restless youngsters at church, the Sunday School is offered. A solemn, faithful, usually female member of the church community would conduct these sessions in indoctrination of the faith with all of the passion he or she could muster on a Sunday morning. Many times the only preparation needed was their faith in God and the desire to do something positive for the church. Their motives were not always readily apparent and many times suspect, but their faith surpassed their shortcomings in logic and education.

Because of their faith they knew what the virtues of life should be and that they were needed to survive the harsh life on this earth, and we had to learn them or perish in Hell. What a message to a developing bundle of neurons. However. very few questions about life were welcome outside the accepted realm of their faith. Faith baby, was their admonition.

Life begins in the warm, secure, encompassing arms of your parents, and excursions to the First Christian Church for me began in the arms of my parents when they carried me to the Sunday services. This Sunday ritual offered them a chance of dressing up in their best clothes and escaping from the uneventful, mundane existence of the daily routine. This break was eagerly looked forward to. A good fellowship was achieved by this mingling of the faithful but even at an early age I questioned the purpose of it and its direction only to be rebuked with a traditional 'faith' admonishment. It's something you feel and believe in when you pray, I was told.

As a child I always welcomed the chance to go to church. It was a fabulously exciting and organized play school for me where toys and activities that weren't to be found at home were made available to me. The church helped quell much of the aggression that had developed in me in the presence of the many rival siblings of the family. Survival is taught and learned early around the playgrounds of life in a working class neighborhood. One learned to establish himself fast or he was run over by the larger ones. You learned your niche in life fast.

*ONE MANS FAMILY............*

# 9
# Lessons learned the hard way.

My father worked hard. My brothers and sisters worked hard at chores around the house and they were always looking for ways to make a little extra money. Starting at the age of four, I shoveled the snow off the walks around the house area even though the snow shovel was almost too big for me to handle.

Early in my life, I realized that I had a great deal of curiosity and the ability to take control of situations, exploit them, and gain understanding that could be used later. I always felt that I had control of my situation or problems and that they would work out if I didn't panic. I picked up the concept that moderation of everything in the long run proved to be the most beneficial course. Don't criticize before everything is known. Use moderation, restraint, and not your mouth right away if you could help it. Eating was good but don't stuff yourself or you'll regret it. Study every day and review well before a test rather than having to do it immediately before a test. If you drank too much you would get sick, but one or two drinks could make a person feel good without the disastrous results of overindulgence. Overindulgence and excessive goals were not compatible with a successful life from my point of view. Moderation produced more desirable results. These things were learned early in life in the free environment of Eighth Avenue.

And I was extremely curious—about everything. Sometimes it seemed I could become obsessed with the most dumb things, and I had to satisfy these curiosities no matter what or how long it took. Take the snow-melt problem. Between the heavy, broad, flat doors and the back porch that led into the kitchen, was a intriguing space five feet wide that captivated me immensely. One day after a snow I decided to use the space as a scientific experiment. It was a very heavy snowfall, so I shoveled paths through the snow to the garage and street sidewalk. As I cleared off the snow on the back porch, a tremendous urge came over me and I began collecting the snow in a pile between this space beside the porch. It wasn't enough. I then gathered snow from along the walks and carried it to the space and continued piling it higher. Mother came out from the kitchen and watched me. "What are you doing?" she asked. "I want to see how long it takes before it is all melted," came the reply. "Why?" mother asked. "Just because,". For some compelling reason, I was curious about finding out the length of time it would take to melt the snow I had piled in this spot. It was the dead of winter and it could take forever; however, the urge to find out was overwhelming and I needed to know. It would be months before I had my answer, but that was all right. I needed to do it, that was all. The exact time it completely melted was not recorded in the Argus Leader. But that's not the important thing about this type of curiosity. It was a significant question to me and I pursued it for a answer. Come to think of it, many extremely important personal events and questions that have real significance to individuals are never recorded in any publication or local newspaper. Changes in society and important events in the history of mankind that were ultimate turning points many times are not deemed important enough at the time of happening to record. Hindsight facilitates this lack of intelligence.

I was a worker. I learned to like to work no matter what it was. Only later in my young life did I grow to understand that if one shoveled a sidewalk or driveway for a neighbor I would get some money for the deed. I learned that if you mowed a lawn you could get paid for it. If you did any type of work that the adult didn't have time to do or didn't want to do, you could expect to get some money for your effort. Each task paid a different amount of money, depending on the amount of effort involved and sometimes it seemed that being a kid helped them make up their mind to help you out.

Or so I thought.

When I was ten years old, I unfortunately found out the hard way that not all adults were fair or trustworthy in their assessment of your worth of work. A case in point.

I was asked by an elderly lady to make a garden for her. The area she showed me was on her adjoining lot and it was in grass but she wanted to remove the grass and plant a garden this spring. It was a large lawn and I knew it would take a lot of effort. I took her at her word when she told me that she would pay well and it would be worth my effort. Respecting her word, I pressed the money issue no further. Knowing it was a number of days worth of hard work, I took a four-prong fork that was as tall as I was and started almost as soon as she had finished talking. I was eager to get the job done and earn some money. In order to take the grass off the old lawn, I had to put the fork under the grass and roll it after breaking it loose from the dirt beneath it. The leverage was difficult for my size but I persisted.

After working diligently for half a day, a neighbor lady to the north of the lot called me over and invited me in when I was taking a break. She gave him some lemonade and a sandwich. As I had not brought any lunch with me, I ate with vigor.

The lady was very nice and we talked after the lunch as she puttered around the brightly-lit kitchen. As I left she cautioned me about making sure that the lady that hired me paid me for my work. I didn't think much of it at the time because I had already been promised money for my time and effort. The first day ended and I went home exhausted but exhilarated at the job I had accomplished the first day. Rising early the next morning, I returned to the yard and went right back to work at getting the soil loose and off the ground. It went slowly and again around noon the lady next door called me over and gave me lunch again. After working all afternoon, I quit to go home but I returned early the next morning again. The job was getting done and I felt that I had only a partial day's work left. I had noticed a number of times when I had glanced at the house that the curtains were slightly open behind the elderly lady's windows and I had caught a glance of her watching me from behind the small opening. This pleased me that she took an interest in my good work and it made me work faster and harder immediately after seeing her. I knew that she knew how diligently and hard I was working so I worked harder when I knew she was watching. She would surely see that I deserved all of the money she would pay me. Lunch again was welcome from the lady to the north and another warning about getting paid from the old lady. Why is she telling me this again, I asked himself as I went back to work. Now I was beginning to become concerned and worry a little about why this lady persisted with this warning.

That afternoon I finished the job.

As I approached the front door to get paid, I felt that I had done a wonderful job for her. I was very excited about the amount of money I would get for all of the hard work. I was confident that I would get a lot of money.

I knocked on the door, and waited. After what seemed like a eternity, the door opened slightly and a clenched fist was thrust out from behind it without a word being said. Proudly I put my palm out toward the fist and it opened. A coin was dropped into my hand and the door was rapidly slammed shut. No "thank you", or comment was forthcoming. No praise for the good job done. Nothing but the coin in my hand remained. I looked at the coin she had dropped into my hand. It was a silver fifty-cent piece. I stared at it in disbelief. After a few puzzled minutes of looking at the coin, I turned and walked off the porch, still looking at the coin, believing that it would somehow change into a silver dollar at least. But no luck. All of the way home I had this really bad feeling that I had been taken by this kindly-looking old lady.

As I looked at the coin in my hand, I actually felt ashamed. What had I done wrong? My pride was sorely hurt. Hadn't I done a good-enough job? I felt like taking the coin back to the lady and giving it back to her. Why? I had earned it, and possibly more, I felt. Maybe she couldn't afford more money. No. She was just cheap, and she had taken advantage of me. That was what hurt. She had taken advantage of me. Next time. Next time...I won't ever let it happen again. The next job I did I would have to make sure that I knew what the person wanted done, and just what the pay would have to be. There was to be no more misunderstanding of my worth.

*WHO KNOWS WHAT EVIL LURKS IN THE MINDS OF MAN?*
*ONLY THE SHADOW KNOWS........................*

# 10
# Teeth, Hair

My mother had all her teeth pulled out and wore false ones by the time she was in her 30s; my father had all of his upper teeth pulled and wore false ones by his 30s; my two sisters have false teeth; my brothers have false teeth. The Midwest is a haven for false teeth makers and dentists that pull teeth.

All babies, such as I was, start off life with roughly the same problem: we don't have any teeth.

Within a few months my 'starter' set appeared, much to the delight of my parents and me. Their development become a point of pride for me, my parents, and grandparents. After the initial excitement of their first arrival, the progress was carefully watched and probed with fingers until all were accounted for.

A child's other bodily functions then become the focus of attention and the teeth are forgotten. Within a few years, however, they again became the focus of attention. The slow progression of loss of baby teeth and the gaining of permanent teeth has been followed with curiosity since time one. The tooth fairy still persists to aid this attainment. Look under the pillow to find your reward of getting a 'new' tooth.

The teeth's looks and position can be a blessing or a bane for life. Too far apart or too close together can develop the child's self consciousness or self confidence. They can not be ignored. To smile or not to develop a smile many times depends on gaps or protruding buck teeth.

In the modern age of the flourishing practices of orthodontists, this problem can be corrected or modified easily.

In the 1930s however, there was never enough money for families like ours to solve this condition. Tooth paste and tooth brushes were a luxury we could not afford either. Teeth were brushed by putting baking soda on you finger and inserting it into your mouth. Your fingers became the brush as it was rubbed across the teeth. This seemingly distasteful practice was the only tooth care afforded by millions of lucky children like me. Children by the millions never even developed this ineffective habit of tooth brushing. Developing the habit of tooth brushing may have been more important at the time than the dentifrice that was put into the mouth. Recently baking soda has been given a new life for brushing teeth.

The expected result of lack of properly brushing teeth and tooth care occurred within a few years. Tooth decay became rampant. Small brown spots occurred at first, but generally ignored by the hapless parents. Dentists were expensive and the use of them minimal. The cavities got larger. The children smiled less and the aches started. It seemed that the pain always occurred on a weekend. At this time, even if the parents wanted to send you to a dentist, they could not. Oil of cloves was pressed onto the cavity with a cotton swab. The intense initial pain masked out the real pain and some relief came for a little while. But the pain came back. After sometimes many days, when it became too great for even the parents to ignore, a dentist appointment was set up.

A visit to a dentist on South Minnesota Avenue was not looked forward to even in the horrible state of pain you were in. After sitting down in his chair and a preliminary look into the mouth to find the culprit tooth was done, the dentist selected a drill and the fun began. Novocaine, although it had been discovered, was not readily available to the general public, on at least not to our dentist. Or maybe it cost too much. Sadly for us, we did not get Novocaine to deaden the drill or the pain. A tooth drilled without Novocaine is a tooth and a mouth that makes you feel very anxious. You body heats up and the tension abounds throughout your body. The drilling sound makes you immediately tense up and when after many more anxious moments the drill finds the nerve........WOW.!! The term 'gutting it out' has real application here. If you were lucky and you had only one cavity, the fast trip out of the dentist's chair was all you could think about. But wait, the crowning ouch of the dentist's visit is about to happen. As you left, the dentist gave you a piece of rich candy for being such a brave child in the chair. A piece of candy! The addition of more cavities began before you got out of the dentist's office. This was the ultimate gift designed to stimulate business—the American way of business.

Luckily, while in my teens, I met a dentist that admonished me when I wanted my teeth pulled to solve further decay and cavities. "They're the only teeth you'll ever have" he said. "Pull them out only as the last resort," was his advice, and I took it.

..............................

There were five boys in the family by the end of the '30s. Boys need less grooming attention than girls. Boys don't care a great deal about their appearance until the age of girl awareness and hormone change, usually in their teens, when their grooming becomes self-conscious and all-important.

Boys begin to emit foul odors after a few days of playing and they need to be bathed, so this is not a good project to scrimp and save money on. Without the modern tub and unlimited hot water available in the house to use, this function was sparingly used and confined to one day a week, usually Saturday night. The younger the boy, the harder it was to even accomplish this feat at least one day a week but the body odor and perseverance of the mother accomplished this handily. Two and sometimes three boys could be bathed in the same water but the older ones balked at the dirty water and fresh warm water would be prepared on the stove while the gray water was thrown out under the trees.

A boy could survive without a bath for days, as it was not a visible thing. Odorous but not visible. Haircuts were another thing. The hair grew and it had to be periodically groomed. The custom was to have fairly short hair unless you were less than five years old. A professional barber cost money, however. To cut five boys' hair at 25 cents each would add up to $l.25 a month. Fourteen loafs of ready-baked store bread could be bought at the grocery store with this much money if we had bought store bread. So with a eye to saving money and the patience of a saint, my father cut our hair. One of the items the Jewel Tea Company carried was home hair-cutting clippers and they came with a comb. A stool was set in the yard when the weather was good. This kept the mess of hair cutting outside and left less for my mother to clean up. If the weather was bad or in the winter the stool was placed in the middle of the kitchen floor where the cutting proceeded. One by one we climbed upon the stool, had a dishcloth draped across our shoulders, and took our turn at getting our hair cut.

The experience was usually pleasant unless our father happened to be irritated for some reason. The hand that squeezes the hair clippers has to be steady and firm or the hair gets pulled. This hurt, and tears would roll down the cheek. Although my father tried to make the hair presentable, it usually looked like it had been cut using a bowl as a guide. The hair on the sides was extremely short and the hair above sometimes uneven but after a few days it always grew back and became presentable.

This hair-cutting ritual continued for me until I was a senior in high school. Then, for the first time in my life, I went to a professional barber to have my hair cut.

*HEN-REEE!*
*HENRY ALDRICH...............*

*Brother Jimmy bundled up for the cold weather. In the background is our family's outhouse. (FF Collection)*

*Target practice with the .22 was a fun thing to do on a Sunday afternoon. (FF Collection)*

# 11

# The teeter-totter, Outhouses, Hunting

The large wooden cupboard was placed in the kitchen by Bill and Dad. Then the dishes, glasses, and cups were placed in it by Mother. It was a large piece of furniture, almost reaching the ceiling. And it was a thing we were told to leave alone. This cupboard was visited regularly by our mother as it was also a convenient place to put things she didn't want the youngsters to have.

At the same time, it was also a place of attraction as us kids. We knew that Mommy put things on the top shelf that she had taken away from us. "Stay away from there," she would say and we walked away trying to figure out a way to return when she wasn't looking. It was a vicious circle, and the cupboard never had an easy day.

The older kids were taller and were not as concerned with what was on the shelves as what role it may play in their quest for fun. Its presence only encouraged an accident that was waiting to happen.

The protruding corner of the shelf of the cupboard proved too much of a temptation one Saturday evening while the folks were next door playing cards with our neighbors. Saturday night card playing was a customary entertainment for our parents which they thoroughly enjoyed. It gave them a chance to get away, but not too far away, and a chance to let their hair down and sometimes have a little libation. Always looking for some new game to play, my six year old sister, June, took a wooden leaf from the large table in the dining room and conjoled her brother, Charles, to help her use the cupboard corner as a balance for the teeter-totter she had fabricated. It took only one 'teeter and one 'totter' before the entire cupboard came crashing down with disastrous results. All the plates, glassware, glasses, and bowls went flying in every direction with a large crash. Everyone was terrified. The noise was heard by our parents with immediate results. They and all the neighbors came running, not knowing what to expect but expecting the worst.

"What's happened in here? What the hell is going on, we heard a loud crash. Oh, my God." And he stopped in mid-stride and with mouth wide open, gasped.

My father was of German heritage and he sometimes vented his anger in powerful ways. Expecting all hell to break loose, the kids ran into their bedrooms to seek the security of their 'night-night' blankets and also distance themselves from the damage and expectedly irate parents. After the initial shock of the scene subsided, the children were checked for injuries but none were found, although the kids were highly agitated. Expecting the wrath of our father, they stayed in the other rooms and peered out the doorway ready to retreat and hide for what they knew would be the worst spanking of their lives. However, lo and behold, the first thing Daddy and our neighbor did was pick up a broom and a shovel and start sweeping up the mess.

"Get that box from the boys' room so we can put these broken dishes into it, Mother. What a mess. Watch out for the glass so you don't get cut, Harold. I'll get the dust pan to put it into the box. Luckily nobody was hurt," he said as he diligently looked around for stray glass to put into the box.

When is he going to hit us? Odd, we thought. We knew we deserved at the least a spanking for this. When is it coming?

The broken glass was put into the cardboard box and carried outside. Just outside of the back door was an abandoned cistern with a large round metal cap on it. The cap was rolled off and the broken glass was thrown into the empty well. To our continued surprise, nothing more was said as our folks walked back to the interrupted card game. The surprise and disappointment of not being punished for this escapade was almost more than the pain would have been had we been spanked. At least we would have gotten rid of our guilt feeling with a spanking.

It took many months before enough of the glass plates and dishes were replaced so we could enjoy a meal without sharing dishes.

..............................

"Take those newspapers from last Sunday to the outhouse when you go. We're almost out of paper."

In the world of outhouses, newspapers were the paper of choice. It was much preferred for outhouse use over the hard, slick paper of the *Time* or *The Saturday Evening Post* magazines, however, they would gladly be pressed into service and used when nothing else was available.

Every house that lacked indoor plumbing, like ours, had to have an 'out house' or privy that was placed somewhere in the back yard. We had a 'two holer' and it was placed way in the back of the lot next to our neighbors property line where the hot stifling summer heat created odors that could not be smelled from the house. The lowered temperature of the winter days lessened the possibility of odors; however, on days below freezing one did not linger very long.

As it was a necessary and well-utilized structure in our life, it had to be moved every few years because the hole beneath it would fill up. A new hole about four by four by six feet had to be dug away from the original site. The new site had to be chosen carefully for health and convenience of weather.

The deliberation as to where to move it was not taken lightly, and it sometimes took many weeks to finally determine where to move it to. We kids started digging a new hole during the week while Dad was working so the privy could be moved on the weekend when Dad was available to help. Carefully it would be tipped over and rolled side over side to the new hole. There it was righted again. Everyone helped and those that were too young to dig and help move it would stand on the sidelines and watch. It was a big important event in the lives of everyone in the family. After the move was completed, everyone just stood for a while to absorb this spectacle of accomplishment.

Winters were a test of man's resolve and the most trying time to use the outhouse. Speed was essential if one was to survive. The fear of freezing to death while doing one's business was uppermost in everyone's mind. There has never been a recorded death of a person freezing to death in a outhouse as far as is known, and you didn't want to be the first.

In the hot days of summer, they could be unbearable for quite the opposite reason.

The kids had a vested interest in building and maintaining a good, solid privy. Especially when Halloween rolled around. This holiday created much interest in your neighbor's privies, especially neighbors that had no children. You didn't tip over your friends privy, only distant neighbors who could not identify you, or so you thought. Usually there was a lot of talk of doing this type of mischief, but it actually very seldom happened in our neighborhood. We were too scared of the consequences of being caught. The thought of fixing and righting another persons privy was not the most pleasant thought. But it was fun fantasizing tipping it over with someone inside.

................................

The cool autumn days in the Heartland brought relief from the months of blistering hot summer sun. The nights were cool and invigorating now. Perfect weather for Dad and us to go road hunting for rabbits. This time of year was especially good because the shortening days of light meant we could use a spot light to freeze the rabbits in their path, giving everyone enough time to take aim before firing the .22 rifle.

Dad told us to be ready by the time he got home from work, around five o'clock. As five o'clock approached, Mom made sandwiches and perked a fresh pot of coffee. He drove into the yard and parked the car. He didn't waste much time as he gulped down a sandwich and took time for a cup of coffee. As Dad ate, a shout from outdoors told him that Bob, our neighbor who was going with us, was ready and waiting by the car. We had the bullets and rifle ready by the door and within minutes we were off for the hunt.

The old Studebaker roared to life. This car had running boards and fenders that were crucial for the successful pursuit of road-rabbit hunting.

"We'll go south of town tonight," Dad said to Bob as he turned south on Cliff Avenue. "Out by the old farm, then drive towards Shindler, then over by the river." Bob nodded his head but said nothing. Dad knew where the best rabbits were hiding.

And we were off in pursuit of rabbits on the outskirts of the town. It took about ten minutes to get to the graveled county roads where we could start hunting. Dad drove the car while in town, but while hunting it took little skill to drive the car down the country roads, so one of the older kids would drive the car slowly while the men hunted. While my older brother Norm drove the car, Dad and his friend, Bob Moffle, would ride on the front fenders of the car to get the best view and shot. Very little talking went on as everyone kept a sharp eye out for rabbits. The car crept slowly along the road.

"Over there," Bob shouted. Everyone strained to look.

"No, only a rock," Dad replied. A lot of false alarms were shouted as seeing the little critters in the ditch along the side of the road was not easy. When a rabbit was actually spotted the men would jump off the fender and rapidly move toward the rabbit, trying not to spook it, all the time raising the .22 rifle, checking the safety to make sure it was ready to fire. POW POW POW went the rapid shots of the .22s blasting out in the cool evening.

"I got him. I got him," someone would yell out as they advanced toward the spot they had fired at. As the forward hunter hurried toward the quarry, the other would jump on the running board grabbing the center post of the doors to hold on and the car would carry him down the road. Norm hadn't learned the art of breaking easily and usually he jerked the car to a stop short or long of the desired spot.

The men were good shots and they got better as the season progressed and more hunting was done.

Sometimes the rabbit had been only wounded and it would crawl away. Then the hunt to find it would begin. Stomping down the tall grass in the side ditches could become monotonous after a while of frustrated search. The rabbits rarely cooperated in being found, but that was part of the hunt. Back and forth in the ditch, over the barbed wire fence to look on the other side of the fence in the fields. After a while, if their luck was bad, they'd give up looking, being convinced that it had not been hit.

This procedure could be repeated a half-dozen times in an evening as the night got darker.

Two or three rabbits was usually enough for the family. The kids didn't eat the critters and Mom didn't like them setting around the house for very many days. Fresh ones could be gotten another night.

The rabbits had to be dressed—a job Mom hated to do and we hated to watch done. Dad sometimes did it, but he hated to do it also. "Tastes just like chicken," I was told. But I didn't eat chicken. Neither did my mother. She didn't like the taste of chicken so that's probably why we kids didn't eat rabbit or chicken. After the rabbits were skinned and gutted, if they were not cooked immediately, they were put in a pan of salt water to take the wild taste out of the meat, and this pan was set in a cool place to be cooked later. It was a thrill to go hunting with the men folk in the cool autumn nights.

..............................

One very memorable event that occurred in this house that will never be forgotten happened on December 31, 1936, when I was almost four years old. Around ten o'clock in the evening a large boom was heard and our house shook frightfully. After a minute of stunned silence, my father, mother with the rest of the family following, rushed out of the house to determine what had happened. My father thought that the roof of our house had exploded for some reason. As they stood in the street looking at our chimney, the other families of the neighborhood were out checking their chimneys and cars and anything else that could have caused this terrible explosion. After being satisfied that it did not have an immediate concern for them, they went back into the home to get out of the cold weather. It was not until the next day that the family found out that the Larson Hardware powderhouse east of town had been blown up by some bank robbers that were trying to kill two members of their gang. These two members, Helen Seilers and Harold Baker of Sioux City had been lured to Sioux Falls by their partners who wanted to do one last job before the gang broke up. Their real intention, however, was to kill Helen and Harold for wanting to get out of the gang so they decided to blow them up at this powderhouse. After thinking they had knocked out Helen and Harold, the four tons of blasting powder and one and one-half tons of dynamite were detonated. In the meantime, Helen had been able to crawl out of the powderhouse to safety and poor Harold was left inside. All that was found of him was a thumb. The sound of the explosion was heard twenty miles to the north in Dell Rapids and over $20,000 of glass was broken in homes and businesses.

..............................

The day was one of those beautifully warm September days. The morning had been cool, but you knew that it would warm up into the 70s by noon. The air was comfortable.

As four of the five children took their place at their accustomed chairs at the oval table in the crowded room that was off to the side of the small kitchen, they suddenly heard Uncle Lawrence's Model T outside in the street. He braked to a stop amid a large squeal of the brakes. His Model T was instantly recognizable by his squeaky brakes. The door to the car slammed shut and we could hear him running to the house.

"Roger's dead," he blurted out as he pulled open the screen door and hurried in. "Car accident on Minnesota Avenue. He was on his way home.... home from school ...for lunch" His breath came in short pants and he stopped and leaned on a chair for support. "It was terrible. Killed instantly by a truck as he crossed the highway. Do you have a drink? I need something to calm my nerves."

Mom knew he needed something to drink. He always did. He drank all of the time. However, she reached into the kitchen cupboard's top shelf and took down a pint of whisky that had been hidden from our sight. I recognized the bottle because Dad had poured a little from it into some tea and had given it to Charles for his cold a week before. Lawrence poured a shot into a glass and downed it immediately. Then he poured another shot in the glass. He continued... "Do you know where Ed is? He might be over at Bill's or Oliver's. Oliver said he had some cabinet work for him to do. This is awful. I'll have to find out where they will take the body, probably Miller Funeral Home but I'll find out for sure. Probably have the funeral Wednesday or Thursday." Another gulp of whiskey was downed but he suddenly realized that all of the kids were watching him and he put the glass and the bottle down.,

All of this had taken only five minutes as he swung around to go out of the door. "I'll go find Ed and tell the rest of the family." Mom knew that he'd be drunk before supper time and probably would not be able to work at Metz tonight. That was expected. Any excuse to drink, she thought. She loved her brother, but his drinking bothered her. Just like his dad, she thought.

The Motel T engine roared down the dirt road in a cloud of lingering dust and it got very quiet in the house again as the kids finished their lunch.

"Mommy, what did he mean, Roger got killed? What's that mean?"

Miller's Funeral Home was an old, well-established funeral home for as long as we could remember. It was the only place we went for funerals. Mr. Miller had started with a livery stable on Main Avenue, across from the high school in the early part of this century. He got started in the funeral business when he was called upon to remove a woman's body from a hotel room downtown. This gave him the idea of starting a parlor to put bodies at while funerals were being set up for people who didn't have a home or anyone to set up the funeral. Most funerals were home affairs yet, whole families would meet and then take the body to the cemetery themselves but the city was changing with a lot of outsiders who didn't have families nearby. He would fill that need. Mrs. Miller took an embalming class and she became the first woman licensed for this business in the state.

A distinctive Spanish style building was built at the corner of Thirteenth and Main. This distinctive architectural sight became the funeral home of our family's choice over the years.

A family funeral was not to be taken lightly in the '30s. All of the immediate family and relatives were contacted immediately to let them know of the loss. A day off work had to be taken by the working men and this was no small decision to take lightly. A day's pay could be lost. All of the relatives would make their greatest effort to attend the funeral no matter how far away they lived. To miss the funeral caused a great deal of distress for the grieving family and it was never forgotten or forgiven unless you had a exceedingly valid excuse. Years later you could be reminded of this fact. Everyone was expected to be there in their finest clothes, and on their best behavior. Old animosities and petty jealousies were expected to be forgotten on this day and there definitely was to be no heated arguments about anything. After the service by a pastor at the funeral home, the impressive car caravan down the city streets with lights on followed and a final burial service at the cemetery occurred. A reception followed at the grieving family's home. All of the women of the families were expected to pitch in and prepare a buffet—nay, a banquet—for the dozens of family and relatives who came from everywhere. It was the biggest social event that I could remember the family having. Family picnics were never this big. The event would last all day and sometimes into the night. The service usually took place in the morning and the meal and social gathering lasted the rest of the day until late afternoon usually. Introductions of new additions to the family occurred, conversations and gossip were caught up on and this all had to take place in a few short hours. Many had not seen each other since the last funeral. The kids played outside quietly with no loud noise or trouble. Any trouble and you had to go sit quietly in the car until you could behave. Drinking by the men was quietly allowed so long as nobody got drunk or rowdy. After the day was over, everyone left for home. There would be no gathering like this again until the next funeral.

*Ghost riders in the sky...........*

*The Sioux Falls Post Office at Twelfth and Phillips was ready for use after expansion in 1933. (Courtesy Center for Western Studies)*

*A paradise for youngsters, Drake Springs was completed in 1934. (Courtesy Center for Western Studies)*

# 12
# Drake Springs Pool, The Circus

It was time for a swim.

Summers could become extremely hot and humid in the Heartland. The heat became suffocating. By eight o'clock it could be over 80 degrees in the shade and by 11 o'clock your limp body didn't care any more. If only the invention of air conditioning would hurry up and happen. It was hot and the afternoon wasn't going to offer any relief. Maybe by sundown it would rain...or we would die.

"Mommy, is it okay if we go swimming at Drake's?" June asked.

"Sure, go ahead. Just be careful, and be back home by four o'clock," Mommy instructed the two girls in front of her. "Are the boys going with you?"

"No, they want to go over the railroad tracks. We want to go over the Cliff Avenue bridge."

"Just be careful."

The muddy Sioux River had, for many years, satisfied the swimming needs for those who wanted a place to swim and get relief from the heat. There were also the numerous abandoned stone quarries and sand pits in the surrounding area that were full of cool, clear water. But these pits of pleasure were sometimes dirty, always unsupervised and extremely dangerous when diving into them. Outcrops of rocks abounded under the surface of the water. In the early 1930s the time had come to seek another solution for the growing number of kids in the community. Being a successful and progressive city now, the need to show the other cities in the Heartland that Sioux Falls cared for its kids became important. A public swimming pool was the solution.

Over one-block square in size, Drake Springs swimming pool, on the east side, was enormous in size. It was built in the early 30s next to Drake's well. Drake's well had been drilled by the pioneer Mr. Drake with the aim of supplying water to the City. The water from it was cold and of the purest type. However, the city fathers decided it would be inadequate after considering the population and projected growth. Finally the city developed another source for its use to the north of town. Clean, cool, and fresh, Drake's springs did produce enough water to supply most of the large one block square size swimming pool. The rest came from the river. The zillions of children that would use it wasn't interested where the water came from, they wanted to swim.

With the idea of thrift in mind, beauty being a secondary thought, the pool was constructed using concrete and the locally obtained pink quartzite

*The circus parade that went down Phillips Avenue offered a preview of the excitement that could be seen that night under the big top. (Courtesy Center for Western Studies)*

stone for the many steps surrounding the pool. The pool was divided into two sections, a deep end for adults and older kids, and a shallower 'kids' part. To enter the pool, you had to step through the cold, milky-looking chlorine-disinfectant water at the entrance. This part of the swimming ritual was done quickly, then you rushed into the pool at the one-foot water depth and embarked on hours of water fun until exhaustion forced us out.

The two sections were divided by a chain strung across the width of the pool at about four feet in depth. Set in the middle of the pool, just across the chain in the deep end, was a lifeguard platform, five or six feet above the water, built around a fifty-foot-tall telephone pole. Only lifeguards were allowed on the stand and they kept an eagle eye on the youngsters. At the deepest part of the pool, about thirteen feet deep, there were three diving boards—two small ones and a very high one. The first jump off the 'high dive' was the greatest thrill of one's young life, especially when some of your friends were watching.

The water was always cool even at the height of the summer season. It was always invigorating and refreshing.

Public transportation cost money. My family avoided it, but the desire to swim was so overwhelming that we walked. In order for me to get to the pool from our home on Eighth Avenue, I had to walk about three miles. The fastest way of getting there was to walk east to Cliff Avenue, north on Cliff Avenue, cross the Sioux River, turn left and there it was. Drake Springs. This route was the route the girls and the smaller children took. However, the older boys being more venturesome, took the railroad tracks route.

There were dangers in the railroad route. Watch out for the cars while crossing the street at Fourteenth, then continue on the tracks to the Sioux River railroad bridge.

The river was over a block wide at this point and you had to use the Great Northern bridge to get across. It lacked a people-walk in the '30s. There was no superstructure above the bed of rails and ties, but there were extra-wide spaces between some ties that led to the cement pillars that held the bridge up. If a train came along as you were crossing, you could climb down between the ties of the rails and wait while the train crossed over above you. Great fun!

The tracks on the bridge across the Sioux River were scary Don't look down at the river, I told myself or you'll get dizzy. After crossing the Great Northern bridge, there was only a short two blocks walk to Drake Springs but this was the hottest part. The walk past the Howard Wood Stadium and the massive Girton Adams river ice storage plant went quickly and you looked for the gate to the lawn of the swimming area. After walking the hot tracks, the first step onto the green grass of the pool grounds by the pump house was like stepping into heaven. The cool grass was enticing. Running for relief from the hot railroad tracks was almost mandatory. Past the Lilly pond we would run, under the trees, down the grassy slope where people lounged and bathed in the sun, and finally the gate to the pool welcomed us. Mrs. Wheeler's always watchful eye made sure we stepped through, not around, the cold milky-white chlorine disinfected water. Finally after the hot two-mile walk, we plunged into the cool water for an afternoon of pleasure.

................................

There were no words that excited me as a youth in Sioux Falls more than 'The circus is in town.' They were magic words. The world was coming to Sioux Falls. The world of excitement, mystery, and fun.

The impending arrival of the circus train had been posted on every telephone pole in the city for the last week with the schedule of the parade that was to follow. The town was alive with excitement. The circus was the biggest event that could visit the town for the entire year and the parade was a welcome break to everyone's routine.

The Milwaukee Road Railroad tracks to the south of town carried the circus train to Sioux Falls. As it approached the siding by the Drake Springs swimming pool, the excitement mounted. Hundreds of people would line the railroad tracks on the East Side to watch its arrival. This would be the home of the circus for the following week. The train slowed to almost a walk as the engineers kept a look out for onlookers and cars that came to watch the activity.

Past the Lilly pond and the Drake Springs swimming pool it inched and finally stopped with a jerk. A momentary silence occurred before steam began pouring out of the side of the steam engine relieving the boiler's pressure.

The doors of the cars swung open. The unloading of the circus began immediately as numbers of roust-abouts poured out of the train. The excitement was contagious. The area became a sea of men and animals as wagons were edged off the flatcars and brightly painted boxcars. Everything was organized. Everyone from the circus knew what he was to do and he did it with shouting and vigor. The unloading of the cars became a show for the townspeople and the 'carnies' were good at putting on a show.

As the animals were unloaded they were lined up and herded toward Franklin Avenue, passing the Howard Wood Stadium. A parade was in the making. The street became completely packed with elephants, horses, clowns, wagons, and circus people. By now the highway traffic on Tenth Street was at a standstill. Soon it would be stopped as the circus parade made its way over the Tenth Street viaduct to the downtown business section via First Avenue. South on First Avenue the procession went to the Fourteenth Street then turned west to Phillips. On Phillips Avenue crowds of onlookers formed at the curbs. The parade would make its way through the business district until it reached Eighth Street. At Eighth Street it then returned to the East Side. The parade was always better than expected and after it had passed, the excitement lasted for hours.

The elephants created the most excitement when they passed. It was interesting to see the huge lumbering creatures being led by the scantily-clad girls carrying only a stick to guide the monsters. What power...and what a sight. Horses were better known, but their gaily-adorned harnesses along with the brightly-colored wagons with lions and tigers in them were enough to make the kids stare. All the time the parade moved through the streets the loud music of a kaleidoscope blasted your eardrums into numbness. It was exciting and everyone wished the Big Top was as ready to go as they were. In some of the earliest visits by the circus the tents were set up by Uncle Bill's home on Southeastern Avenue, below the Mount Pleasant Cemetery area.

..............................

The circus had arrived in Sioux Falls. Franklin and Eighth Street was used in later years for the tents and show, but in earlier years it set up on vacant land not far from the Cherry Rock Bridge. I remember both places well. Either place caused the same awe and wonderment in the townspeople. After the parade down the main streets of the business district, the tents had to be set up. This was as much an event to watch as the parade for those who could spare the time to watch. Setting up the tent caused a crowd to gather to watch the well-trained elephants pull the ropes on the pulley that lifted the Big Top up a center pole about thirty feet. Two or three of these poles supported the heavy tents for the performances along with the smaller poles around the sides. This is where the excitement and activity beyond belief for the kids hit a pitch for the few hours that the circus was being set up. Everything was so organized and everything was happening at once, much to our dismay because we wanted to see it all. What a world. We couldn't get enough of it.

And tonight after all of this commotion had died down, the show would begin for those who could get tickets. The first show was the best, but if you missed the first one, there would be more tomorrow—one in the afternoon as well as one in the evening.

All over the town one could see 'carnies'. Unfortunately, they came with a reputation that was somewhat unsavory. The businessmen hated them and were very careful and watchful when they came into their shop. Their reputation as 'fast talkers' followed them everywhere. Many of the businessmen felt that their mistrust was warranted as these men of the world, the carnies, knew how to cheat and 'fast talk' the 'hicks' before they could catch them at it.

'Count the change twice, *twice*! and don't make change for them if they don't buy anything, they'll cheat you before you know it. Don't trust them. They can charm you out of your watch before you know it.' I heard one of the businessmen admonish his help at a gas station near where the circus set up.

Whether or not this attitude was warranted I never found out and I never had any reason to mistrust the "carnies".

Within a day or two, the tents came down, the circus packed up all its gear, and left us with only good memories. The town again became quiet, actually dull, and we tried in vain to find something that excited us as much as the circus had.

In later years, the advent of TV jaded our wonderment and adventure about the circus. The circus's arrival became less glamorous and its size was cut back to a point of obscurity. The parades ceased and everything was confined to one tent and only a couple of days' stay in a town. A long tradition had been replaced by electronic devices and gadgets that gave very little real excitement back to the child.

*The things we did last summer..........*

# 13
# Fall-Winter-Spring Lilacs

Best of all, I remember the fall as a boy in Sioux Falls.

As the days became shorter and cooler the leaves started losing their green sheen. I knew the time had come for them to start changing color and they would start to fall to the ground. At first the ash trees would start to exhibit this browning and then burst into the bright yellow colors. The time had come. They fell like rain at times, not a hard rain but a gentle one every time a slight breeze stirred them.

Some leaves persisted longer than others. Not all of the leaves of the tree would drop at once with reason known only to God. It was interesting to sit and watch them and speculate about how long it would be before they all would fall. They accumulated in a round pattern on the ground and they piled up high enough for you to walk through them and kick them high into the air. If the accumulation was not high enough you picked up only a few with your exaggerated kick and only a few would go flying.

As they kept falling, it became painfully obvious that the time would come when they would have to be raked. This many times unpleasant chore that fell to the kids stopped you from playing with the other kids in the neighborhood for a while and made you feel like a martyr. But their time would come, you knew. The leaves were to be raked into piles and taken to the street in front of the house and burned when the wind was mild. As we had only a large metal rake with large prongs to rake the leaves, it was difficult to evenly rake the leaves in the grass, as the prongs kept catching when it dug too deeply into the grass. Pain many times was produced by this action of the rake. When the rake rubbed between your thumb and finger, blisters eventually would appear. You hoped they would not break, but they did. When this happened the loose skin would continue to rub your sore and create more sores. This type of pain was not pleasant, especially since it was in the fingers. Every time you clinched your fist or flexed your hand, you were reminded of the sores.

The piles of leaves were too great a temptation for some of the kids wandering down the street. An irresistible urge would suddenly overcome even the most disciplined kid and a fast dash through the pile, kicking the leaves high, and a scurrying fast retreat would ensue. This usually happened so fast that the raker didn't have time to stop it. The pile would have to be raked again. After endless, monotonous strokes with the rake on the grass, the leaves were piled up and taken to the gutter of the street and piled high. The most fun to the kids was about to begin. It was time to put a match to them and burn them. Caution had to be used, though, and any slight breeze could scatter the fire and send it onto the neighbors unraked leaves, or worse start a house on fire. Many times this part was left to adults or they would supervise the burning of the leaves.

The smell of freshly burning leaves was exhilarating. Slowly a blue haze would settle low in the neighborhood and it was disturbed only when a car drove past or someone walked through it. The cool temperature was suddenly made welcome by the warmth of the fire and a strange stillness crept over the neighborhood. One was mesmerized by the warmth and the glow of the fire. All problems were forgotten and one wished that this feeling would go on forever. The adding of unburned leaves to the fire was met with a renewed burst of warmth. The evening slowly lost its light and the red glow of the leaves waned into a small red core of embers. These finally went out and one could feel the cool of the evening again. It was time to go into the house.

................................

The hot summer days drifted into the mild days and cool nights of fall. After fall came what everyone dreaded—WINTER.

Cold mornings are invigorating to say the least. Kids dread them. It meant stepping out of a nice cozy, warm womb environment onto the cold floor of reality. I didn't like the reality either. The first step was the worst experience imaginable, like a cold bucket of water thrown in you face on a hot summer day. The second and succeeding steps were body numbing but tolerable until the pants and socks were pulled on in front of the pot bellied stove that Dad had to get up earlier and stoke. The howl of the wind outside let you know that the worst was yet to come.

Oatmeal made in a large aluminum pot was the waking-up fare in the winter mornings. Sugar and milk helped get the gray goo down the mouth with the least time spent in the mouth as was possible. If the oatmeal was not eaten soon after it was made, it got lumpy and stuck to the aluminum pot's side and bottom and it came out even more difficult in larger lumps. Saturdays and Sundays offered relief from this type of school-day fare as my mother or father could take more time and make pancakes. Their golden-brown color and rich texture as they came off of the griddle made the mouth water. Smothered in butter and syrup and stacked two or three high, it gave one the feeling of being on top of the world. They were very satisfying to us...even more so when we had sausage or bacon to go with them.

When the temperature outside really dipped low during the night, it caused my father a great deal of anxiety, as he had to get the car started to drive to work. The first turn of the key could quickly produce relief if the engine turned over only a few turns and started. This is the way it usually happened but the first anxious moments before starting always persisted. If the first turns of the engine didn't do it, chances are that it meant a long, cold walk to work would follow. When it started, it was left to run as Dad returned to the house to let it get warmed up before the trip to work. Huge white clouds of exhaust kept us informed that the engine was still running. Sitting on a bone-chilling cold car seat has to be the least desired experience needed in life. Even after the engine started, unless a piece of cardboard was put over the front of the radiator to help keep the cold out, it still took five to ten minutes to heat the engine's water. Without this hot water, the heater wouldn't put out enough warmth to come close to being comfortable. Usually the heater didn't work correctly anyway to produce the desired amount of heat for comfort—it was usually too hot or too cold. You never knew what its temperature would be.

Another further drawback, as if we needed one on a cold morning, was the annoyance of warm breath everyone produced. If you happen to breathe onto the windshield, the moisture froze to it and your visibility decreased greatly. You held your breath and breathed away from the front of the car windows as long as you could. All types of gadgets were tried to solve this condition, but many times they exacerbated the problem. One particular gadget product I remember my father trying was a plastic sheet that was sealed on the inside of the car windshield. The principle behind this was to create a dead air space that had no moisture in it to freeze. You were never sure of success until it got cold again and then it was too late to correct the problem until warm weather came...many months later, usually.

When this method was unsuccessful and the defroster didn't work, the struggle to see the road as you were driving was almost comical. You would have laughed if it hadn't been so serious and dangerous. With windows rolled down as you approached the street corners you almost froze to death as the blast of cold air rushed into the open window until the corner was passed and the window rolled up again. This had to be repeated at every approach to a corner. Then you had to lean almost to the windshield to gain access to any spot of visibility that wasn't frosted over. The defrosted spot started at the bottom of the windshield worked its way up eventually. It usually cleared the windshield by the time you got to where you were going.

Winter did, however, provide snow. Snow that had to be shoveled in order to allow access to the outhouse, car, and the streets that were now used as sidewalks. Naturally sledding followed. Sometimes a sled would be tied to the rear bumper of dad's car and one of the children, usually Norman, as he was older, would be allowed to ride from Seventh Avenue to Grandma's house on Third Avenue. Dad didn't drive very fast when he did this. Just fast enough to let the cold air and snow blow in his face and almost freeze him to death. What a thrill!

..............................

The kitchen sink was underneath the west facing window. Mom was idly washing dishes and day dreaming about spring and the warm weather it promised.

The time—the spring of 1939. Every spring created an exciting feeling that was hard to describe—a time of expected renewal. This spring, however, was different.

In 1933 the family, consisting of mom, dad, and five children, had moved into a wooden, two-bedroom house at Seventeenth Street and Eighth Avenue. It was a tight fit for this large family, but they adjusted beautifully to the home and working-class, rural-like neighborhood.

The streets were unpaved in this section of Sioux Falls. There was city water, but no sewer service yet. An 'outhouse' in the back yard was a necessity.

My dad had been extremely fortunate. He had gotten a job at the Sioux Falls Paint and Glass Company shortly after moving here in 1933. Then the economy sank lower. Due to the hard times he had to take a cut in salary from $25 to $15, but at least he had a job and salary that could help our family survive. Times were improving though. He was now making more money and life was easier. The only dark cloud on the horizon concerned what a man named Hitler was doing in Europe. Rumor was that we might go to war.

My mother knew that with the help of God, the determination and hard work of the family, their thrift, and vegetable garden, they could survive the depression.

Spring was here. The sun shone, the snow was gone. The birds returned and the leaves appeared on the trees again. Every spring created an exciting feeling that was hard to describe—a time of expected renewal. This spring, however, was to be different.

A six-foot-tall branching lilac bush stood dormant about fifteen feet from the kitchen window in the back yard. It still had a stand of snow beneath its branches that was slowly being melted by the sun. It had accumulated from a surprise snowstorm that occurred two weeks ago and had taken the town completely by surprise. A last gasp of winter to show the people that nature was still in charge of the prairie. Soon the snow would be gone and leaves would be budding. Beautifully dark, lush, green leaves would be following the buds and then the violet—purple lilac flowers would appear. The subdued violet color was gorgeous—and the sweet smell of the perfume heavenly.

As Mom ran her hands down the front of her apron to dry them, she could feel the slight bulge around the waist of her body. Soon she would need to start wearing a larger smock and then she would not be able to hide her condition. A condition the doctor had warned she should not get into again. Something was not right, he had said, and she should not have any more children. That was the reason she was so tired all of the time. He didn't know exactly what the trouble was, but she should not have any more children. She should save her strength for the children she already had.

Spring is coming and it will be getting warm and beautiful outside, and she was ready for it.

*Every time it rains it rains pennies from heaven*
*Don't you know every cloud contains pennies from heaven..........*

*My family and I moved into my Grandmother's house on Third Avenue in the early 1940's. (FF Collection)*

# 14

# The move to Third Avenue-Galesburg

"Hey, Farmer Jones, what are you doing?" Speed yelled out as he passed by the house. I waved and shouted 'Hi." The kid passing he house was called 'Speed' because he was quick. He could outrun everyone on the block. Speed kept walking up the street and disappeared.

It was a warm afternoon as I sat pensively looking at the street in front of me. The seat I was using as a chair was a pile of boxes and clothes that has seen better days. Apparently they were to be thrown out but Mom hadn't been well lately, so they sat on the front porch waiting for their fate. Her bed had been moved into the front room where she could be tended to easier by the children who were in the house. All of this was going through my head as I sat comfortably viewing the scene from the screened-in front porch on Third Avenue. The screens of the full-length porch had numerous tears in them and a few places had been sewn together by string. The porch needed a coat of paint, though. The whole house needed a coat of paint. Dad was too busy working to even paint the house. But it was a good feeling sitting on the porch looking out at the street scene. The air was still and warm with no breeze giving the slightest relief from the heat. A few beads of sweat were forming on my neck, but it didn't bother me. I was used to a lot more heat. The past week I had been on the Entrim farm to the east of Rowena and it had been in the 90s then, so I was used to the heat.

From the front porch I could see a poster hanging from the tree in front of Mrs. Goldie's house. She's at it again, I thought. The pioneer West produced many hard drinkers and alcoholics. Conditions were far from comfortable and coupled with this the country did not have a lot of cash money floating around. Jobs that gave a man a lot of dignity by earning cash money were hard to find. Wages were low and coupled with the large families in many marriages, this put a great strain on the man of the house to adequately feed and clothe a large family. Many could not afford what we now call the basics necessary to live a normal life. All communities in the West abounded in businesses that would satisfy the cheapest way out of this depressing life and loathsome situation, if only for a few hours. Liquor stores and bars many times outnumbered other businesses in the young western towns. It was also inevitable that the philosophy of the church would clash with the drinking of alcohol. It did because the word of God was not compatible. Drinking was looked upon as a grave weakness and a sin put on earth by the Devil. It was wrong to drink and it was not to be condoned by church-going members. It had to be eliminated. The Women's Christian Temperance Union and other organizations sprang up to counteract and correct this problem. Well-meaning women and men held meetings in their homes to teach especially the young of the evils of drinking alcohol in any form. Any and all forms of drinking were wrong. Articles of advertisements in magazines were to be cut out whenever you had the opportunity. You were never, never, to drink alcohol or you would become an alcoholic and ruin your life and bring shame to your family. 'Lips that touch liquor will never touch mine'. When the meetings for the kids were finished at Mrs. Goldie's house, milk and cookies were served. Thousands of such meetings were held throughout the United States by the W.C.T.U. members.

..............................

As the Sioux River flows south, meandering its way to its rendezvous with the Missouri River, it becomes temporarily sidetracked in an area where the Mesozoic Quartzite rock is exposed in southern South Dakota. The resistance of the land detours the Sioux into an almost full circle so that its southern waters flow east and then north again before being detoured again to the east and finally south toward the mighty Missouri. Over the millennia, the quirk of nature that produced this almost-oxbow configuration slowed the water down to make its turn and in the process deposited alluvium that made the ground flat and fertile in this broad valley that was produced. The high ground in the center of the oxbow became a bulwark of resistance and stands like a medieval castle guarding the surrounding area. This commanding position overlooking the Sioux offered a refuge from the rampages of the Sioux after initial settlement on the lower flood plain was accomplished in the mid-1800s by the Dakota Land Company and the Western Town Company. The thrust of development near the exposed quartzite falls was short lived, as Dr. J. L Phillips bought, laid claim to, and platted the quarter section of the former army barracks area to the south and carved the outline for future development of the downtown business area. In the late 1860s a town was beginning to manifest itself as stores, land offices, and living quarters were developed.

To the south of J.L. Phillips claim, four hundred acres of land was claimed by the successful relator and merchant from St. Paul, Artemas Gale. This gently rolling land, bounded on the north by Twelfth Street, had its southern boundary at Eighteenth Street, thence from Minnesota Avenue to approximately Seventh Avenue. Dirt-lined Phillips Avenue had a gentle grade from the downtown center where William Van Eps had erected his combination store and home and where Harry Corson was building a hotel at Ninth and Phillips. Mr. Gale proceeded to build an elegant home a respectable walking distance from the bustling downtown at about Fourteenth and Phillips. He then laid out streets and homesites for his property and called it "Gales Addition." It became known as "Galesburg".

With the Civil War over only a short time ago, he and many Realtors marveled at the idea of all the issued-out soldiers moving to the west where there was free or pitifully cheap land. The severe economic depression in 1873 stymied the one improvement to Sioux Falls that they knew was a necessity to fully developing the commerce potential of the area—a railroad. The railroad to Worthington, Minnesota, lay only a tantalizingly short distance to the east from the city but it and others were needed to run into the city itself. The transportation potential of the railroads in the 1870s can not be underestimated. Roads were passable but made up of dirt in the summer, but they became a quagmire of mud when it rained. A dependable mode of transportation for lumber and other goods was needed. Artemus Gale continued to lay out the land he had bought for homesites. The sites sold slowly until finally, in 1878, a train steamed into the city. In 1879, the Chicago, St. Paul, Minneapolis, and Omaha Railroad was constructed through the Gales Addition, giving an additional boost to the importance of his acreage. Something more was needed, however. The acreage needed an additional selling point and that came in the form of the All Saints School for girls. This school was built in the Addition on a five acre lot on Eighteenth Street between Dakota and Phillips. It was constructed of Sioux quartzite, as was the Post Office that was built in 1895 at the corner of Twelfth and Phillips. Just a block to the west of the Post Office, bordering the Gales Addition, the Central High School had been constructed, but it was rapidly becoming overcrowded. In 1895 Eleventh and Spring became the site of the newly constructed Irving High School (later renamed McKinley High School). The

*The Galesburg 'gang' is ready for play at the Third Avenue house.*

*City kids need trips to the farm to learn about the animals. (D. E. Fredricks personal collection)*

*Milk, eggs, and meat could be purchased while on visit to the Edwards farm. (FF Collection)*

high school stood her for the next thirteen years until a quartzite high school would be built next to the still standing old Central High School building on Main Avenue. In 1889, one block south of the Central High School site, the Galesburg Addition acquired the Calvary Episcopal Cathedral at the southeast corner of Thirteenth and Phillips. This give to the Addition the third most prestigious reason for living in this area. Again, the durable quartzite rock was used for its construction of the church and it still persists today. But it wasn't until the turn of the century that the greatest influx of settlers came to the area and built in the Gales Addition.

The most desirable area of the Gales' Addition was the western part, between Minnesota Avenue and Second Avenue. This area was close to the convenience of the downtown. It experienced a hub-bub of building activity early on with the construction of bungalows, and one and one-half story gabled cottages—the choice of Sioux Falls' aspiring middle class.

Although the western Galesburg section was developed early, the building of houses in eastern section, around Seventh, Sixth, Fifth, and Fourth Avenues lagged and the homes built were considerably less expensive. Dirt streets, railroad tracks cutting through the section, and nearness of the Sioux River may have made it less desirable. The 'working class' who were frugal with their money bought lots in this area and built their own houses.

The development of the area became less extensive as you progressed eastward and the acreage along the Seventh Avenue border south of General Beadle School (originally Longfellow School until 1925) continued to be used for farming by the Sachen family into the 1940s.

Unique zoning rules allowed the development of a number of grocery stores that were endemic to the area. Just north of the railroad tracks Fred Hyatt's Grocery Store was both a business and a residence at 738 First Avenue. Mr. Loomis had a store only a block to the east at 727 Second Avenue. At Fourteenth and Fourth Avenue George Zimmerman ran a store with James DeZotell at 419 Fourth, only a block to the north. Floyd Gilbranson ran his grocery store across from the Beadle School at Fourteenth and Seventh Avenue. These grocery stores lent a cohesion to the community by their personal service to the mainly working-class residents who could be helped with grants of credit during lean times. The people in the Gales Addition did not have adequate transportation that would allow them to frequent the bigger grocery stores that were developing in the business section of the city many blocks away, so the 'mom and pop' stores near them thrived.. This situation changed in the '40s and '50s and the small grocery stores closed.

In addition to the grocery stores, the Galesburg section had a number of businesses like Girton Adams Ice between First and Second next to the tracks, Polar Cold Storage on Thirteenth Avenue next to the tracks, and a farm-implement business along the tracks to the south of Fifth and Fourteenth.

General Beadle School had been built at the corner of Seventh and Fourteenth. It was to serve this lower economic area; however, the growth toward the McKennan and the Boulevard Addition just south of Gales Addition prompted the school board to authorize the construction of a 'new' Longfellow Elementary School in 1916. This school was built just out of the Gales Addition and only a few blocks from the 1911-built McKennan Hospital.

Economics is a hard fact of life. If you have money, life is sweet. If you don't have money, you must adjust and make the best of your situation. The area east of Second Avenue was known as 'working class' neighborhoods and many of the children learned early in their childhood that life could be especially harder for them. The did not have the money to live as others in their town did. Life was a constant struggle just for their parents to put food on the table. Frustration formed one's life. Sayings and speech were picked up that were frowned on by the surrounding families. Swearing was common and the kids picked it up rapidly. Aggressive behavior was the mode of the day. You learned to look out for yourself on the streets as we were taught that nobody but your buddies would take your side. Lessons of survival were learned early and never forgotten. It was at times a little rough, but I survived.

This attitude of society perplexed and galled me. Hell, I was only expressing myself verbally as playmates and I in the Galesburg area had always done. That was our nature and the best way we had learned to keep the lid on our physical aggressiveness was by vocalizing. Vocalizing was the outlet for our aggression. In the Galesburg it wasn't 'bad' language—it was *our* language. Slowly it began to dawn on me that the area I had grown up in was considered a 'rough' and uncouth area by many of the citizens of the city. I lived on the "wrong side of the railroad tracks." Differences were becoming more apparent now that I was growing up.

..............................

My family and I had moved to 763 South Third Avenue in 1940. My grandfather had bought the two-story wooden house in 1919 when his family had moved off the farm northeast of town by the Brandon Road. This land was later acquired by the city and a sewer plant now occupies the site. Grandpa had died in 1928 but grandma had continued living here with her granddaughter Evelyn. In 1940 Grandma broke her hip and had to go into a nursing home. My family moved into the house from Eighth Avenue. The house was twice as large as the Eighth Avenue house and it was within walking distance to the downtown area. It was built in the late 1880s.

"Mother, we now have a large bedroom, away from the kids," Elmer said to his wife.

"And a toilet. I've always wanted an indoor toilet."

The one bedroom on the first floor was taken over by the parents. There was a porch on the front of the house and the door off the front porch led into a front room that had a pot-bellied stove for heating in the middle of it. A dining room was behind it where the large oak dining table was placed and dominated the room. The table was memorable in that it had lion-paw legs that supported it. When we were little we liked to pretend the lion was stalking us and it was going to get us and eat us up. It was a very terrifying piece of furniture to a youngster. Off the dining room was a room that had been converted into a toilet when sewers became available to the homes in this area. An indoor toilet! We had no shower or tub, though, and the small kids still had to use the large copper tub for their baths. A outhouse originally took care of the needs of the family in this previous farmland. The kitchen was to the rear of the house and in it was another iron wood-burning stove that was used for cooking and heating. Behind this stove was a large enough space for the kids to crawl behind and get warm on cold mornings. All of the kitchen activity centered around this stove, especially on Mondays. Monday was always fondly remembered as 'bean' day.

The yard in front had a little grass, but the back yard consisted entirely of weeds. A shed sat by the alley where the car could be parked occasionally and corncobs stored. The corncobs provided a hot fire in the stove.

From the porch I could view the entire neighborhood without being seen by anyone because of the dark screens. I always had liked being an observer of activities and I especially liked sitting this way on the porch and watching the goings on of the neighborhood, especially when I felt a little down and melancholy like I was right now. I wanted to still be on the farm, running like I did last week. It was so perfect being the only kid out there and not having any brothers or sisters to bother with.

Suddenly a car passed in front of the house. There wasn't much traffic on the street and any car was noticed by almost everyone.

His car wasn't in the driveway, so I knew Mr. Toungie was working at his service station on the East Side. Everybody in the neighborhood knew when he got home, as he roared into his driveway in his Graham automobile and screeched to a halt only inches from his garage. Someday he's going to hit it. Man, he drove that car fast. And it was such a big car. Someday I would have a bigger and better car.

The little one-story house to the north of the Toungie family seemed out of place in the neighborhood as it was a lot smaller than the other houses that were all two-storied, larger family homes. A tragic event had just happened earlier this summer when the mother of the family living in it sent her children to the store to buy a loaf of bread and then when they had left she went into the garage and hanged herself. The shock was still being felt by the neighborhood. Nobody around knew she had been so depressed as to do this. Everything had looked normal with her and the kids played with everyone ever since they had moved in the year before. Sad, and strange, everyone thought. Nobody had a clew that she was this despondent and would kill herself.

The Houge family lived in the two-story white, wooden house to the north of our house. The upstairs was an apartment that had been rented to my grandmother. I liked to go over and see her and play a hand of cards with her if she wasn't embroidering or crocheting. She always got so mad when I beat her at cards, which wasn't very often.

Directly across the street from our house is where a street light hung from a pole. Hours and hours were spent under and around this fixture. At nights we and the neighborhood kids played kick-the-can, hide-and-go-seek, or just plain gathered around to talk. Nobody was around to play anything today. Wonder where everybody was?

...............................

A corner of the kitchen led into a set of stairs to the second floor.. There were three rooms on the second floor—two very large and one small one. One of the large rooms had been used as a kitchen for the renters but now we converted it into a boy's bedroom. The other large room was used as a bedroom with two large double beds put into it. Off of the side of this room was a smaller, more personal room that my older sister used as her bedroom.

From the rear boys' bedroom a view of All Saints School could be discerned and the window allowed us to crawl out on the roof, a thing my father didn't like us to do, but we did it anyway.

One day I climbed out on the roof, put on a make-shift parachute I had sewed together from gunny sacks and jumped off the roof. The only thing that prevented me from being killed by the fall was that the lines of the parachute got caught around a pipe on the roof and this stopped me from hitting the ground with full force. I never tried again to experience the thrill of a parachute jump.

The rear of the lot was large and sloped down to a seldom used alley between Second and Third Avenues. In the spring the melt from the snow would collect in this low spot and flood out the back garage that was by the alley. This water created a wonderful playground for the boys who would build rafts to play on. When a freeze occurred it became an ice-skating pond.

The dirt-walled, dirt floored unfinished basement had no windows. It must have been dug after the house was built, as the foundation of the house didn't extend very far below the floor of the house. One end of it was used for coal storage and the opposite end was used for storage of canned food. The only way to get to it was by lifting a hinged door that was built into the floor. It was eerie going into the basement. Only one light hung from the ceiling and it gave off a ghostly yellow glow. Lack of light made it an unappealing to go into unless it was necessary. Although there was no food open to eat, an occasional rat would visit the cellar and the thought of it would scare the daylights out of us.

There were two beautiful, mature elm trees on the lot. One stood close to the Jones' house to the south, and the kids had built a tree-house in the crotch of the tree. Many hours had to have been spent hauling the lumber up to about the second floor level of their house. A triangular foundation for the cross planks had been built into the tree crotch before it was steady enough to use. A masterpiece of construction—and now it was mine.

The move to Third Avenue was especially good for me. The streets and sidewalks on Third Avenue were paved. This presented opportunity for me. I now could shovel snow for money in the winter. Up before dawn, I would take my shovel in hand and walk the streets looking for lights on in a house. At first it was hard working up courage to ask people to buy things or do work for them, but I got over this shyness fast and now I knocked on doors like a professional Fuller Brush man. I could shovel two or three houses before I went to school. And I had money now. To keep my money safe, I hid it in a jar in the basement, over by the coal bin. Nobody could find it over there because it was too dark. Many of my snow-shoveling customers would buy the Sperry-Moorse seeds that I sold in the spring. The seeds would be sent through the mail in time for the spring seeding of their gardens. A little extra change could be made selling them as well as the potholders my grandmas made to sell. The doilies and potholders sold well to the ladies of this and surrounding neighborhoods.

In the summer there were lots of lawns that I could mow to earn money. My diligence and dependability assured repeat customers throughout the summer.

*Going to take a sentimental journey..............*

Kimball Marinette • Carol Mashek • Don Masker • Patty Masters • Bill Mathers • Norman Mauseth • Howard McCabe • Mickey McDowell • Evelyn Clark McGee • Tom McIntyre • George McKeon • Tom McKeon • Jim John McLaughlin • Joy Bishop Mehlhaff • Dick Don Merrill • Bob Meyers • Jean Sorgdrager • Maxine Brewer Miller • Verna Sachen Miller • Toni Nickelson Milstead • Jim Minick • Janet Picasso Missner • Wanda Mitchell • Harry Mitchell • Darrell Don Modica • George Alice Art Myrtle Helen Mildred Lester Esther Mofle • Robert Esther Lyle Harold Girt Shirley Mofle • Joyce Moon • Hill Audrey Larry Monger • Jim Monick • Kent Morstad • Wayne Mortrude • Donna Murray • Dan Nachel • Bob Gene Sam Tim Nash • Robert Naylor • Harry Neely • Dick Ron Neish • Jack Nelson • John Nelson • Wesley Nelson • Jean Nessan • Marlow Newberger • Jack Neuroth • Ben Bob Newcomb • Ken Noel • John Norberg • Mildred Becker Nuffer • Betty Olson • Bud Gordon Olson • Verlyn Oveson • Melva Anderson Palmer • Delores Lehman Parker • Rose Parker • Ethel Parks • Kay Pasco • Max Pasley • Shirley Paul • Dave Paulson • Dale Paulson • Warren Pay • John Peckham • Joan Lehman Pederson • Evelyn Harvey Pelley • Edna Ostrosky Perryman • George Edna Peterson • Maxine Hansen Peterson • Patricia Petersen • Sam Pfeifer • Inez Pitchford • Denny Dale Plooster • George Poletes • Bill Lavon Polzien • Grace John Carol Edward Patricia Dianne Kenneth Powderly • Vivian Prouty • Lemta Groos Floyd Prouty • Parker Powell • June Lehman Ranney • Hugh Ranney • Bill Ranney • Noreen Canfield Reese • Dick Reid • Ray Reiners • Marcine Reiners • Donna Tyler Reit • Don Renner • Ronnie Richardson • Don Harold Ritter • Dan Robar • Ed Roberts • Jim Tom Robertson • Chad Rogers • Leona Ohlman Rohrer • Dick Ronken • Gloria Bradley Rose • Henretta Floren Jack Jerald Lewis Richard Thomas Rose • Ruth Rote • Dorothy Wilson Rupp • Curt Ruud • Lillian Berreth Betty Coulter Verna Miller George Hank Sachen • Pamela Schuldt Sampson • Darrell Schrader • Delores Schuldt • Bob Dick Duane Ken Les Schuldt • Helen Sorgdrager Schultz • Irene Conklin Schurman • Joyce Scollon • Clayton Wayne Scott • Ted Scott • Jerry Scott • Hazel Seloover • Chub Eddie Harold Shafer • John Simko • Bill Chuck Robert Cora Simpson • Dale Don Vern Skadsen • Esther Skadsen • Lora M Skaff • Jim Skaggs • Dick Skrondahl • Eleanor Small • Alonzo Smith • Bonnie Smith • David Smith • Maxine Clark Snook • Darrel Kenneth Snook • Dean Songstad • Ruth Engles Songstad • Evelyn Kraft Jean Miller Helen Schultz Ernestine DePew Roger Sorgdrager • Dollie Stearns Spade • Dick Spear • Byron Gordon Jim Wayne Spars • Beulah Davis Spielman • Charles Stadtfeld • Daniel Jimmy Pat Virginia Sally Mary Loretta Bill Francis Stanton • Mildred Starnes • Stub Starnes • David Stavig • Bud Monte Dolly Babe Stearns • Bob Steensma • Sandy Stenson • Ron Stephens • Ellen Engles Basche Stephenson • Bill Stockstad • *(continued on page 106)*

# 15

# Raft, Railroad Tracks, Baseball,

Sitting on the muddy bank of the Sioux River at the foot of Twelfth Street we watched the river lazily drift by. As I watched, I mentally clocked the stick I had thrown into the river. It landed half-way across the river. The stick moved slowly, too slowly. The river was too wide to get the stick to the other shore although I had already tried three times to do it. The stick bobbed up and down before settling down to a journey to the falls a few miles away. I had seen the falls and I wondered how long would it take to get there. I threw in another stick to accompany the first. A turtle poked his head out from under the willows by the shore then dove under the water when he saw the kids. "Looked like a snapping turtle," I thought. "Oh, how I hate them." Last week a man that was fishing up by the Rock Island bridge got up to leave, pulled the fish he had caught out of the water, and all that was hanging on the line was the fishs' heads. A snapping turtle had made a meal of the rest of the fish as fast as the man could catch them. I shuddered as I thought of my foot and toes that had been hanging in the water a few minutes ago.

One of the greatest pleasures for me was to play in or around the river—it provided continuous and unlimited exploratory opportunities. Fishing was fun but my family never ate the fish for some reason. The reputation we had heard of the carp as a 'garbage fish' may account for some of the reluctance we had to eat them. We caught them and then threw them back into the water to be caught again by someone else. Also the unpleasant process of preparing them for cooking turned me off. We never ate them.

Swimming in the river was fun, but the fear of the unknown beneath the surface scared us all too much. The dirty, murky water made this unknown a place to be feared. I also knew that snapper turtles were living in the river and that bothered me. If it was possible to swim without touching or walking on the muddy or slimy bottom of the river it would have been tolerable, but this was seldom possible. Needless to say, swimming in the river was kept to a few curiosity attempts by me and then given up. The public pool at Drake Springs was preferable for swimming. Our family had a modern washing machine so we had no need to use it for washing clothes. And city drinking water was available that was cleaner than the muddy river water.

Use of the river as transportation was a fascinating prospect. Mankind had used them for centuries, nay millennia. They were the first highways of America. Lewis and Clark explored the western country using them. The myriad methods that were employed to utilize the power and convenience of the water—sailboats, canoes, barges, paddle boats, and rafts, were a fascinating study. How often I had stood on the shore and wished there was a way to get onto the river and sail away. But I had no sailboat, canoe, barge, paddle boat, or raft.

Of all these choices the only one possibly attainable was a raft. A raft could be easy to make, if you had the materials to make it. There was lumber at home, but it was over a mile from the river. It could be carried to the river piece by piece and put together into a raft, but that would take a lot of time and work.

I kept thinking about this idea. Five or six guys from the neighborhood would be needed if the raft was built at home and carried to the river. That was a lot of work. Better to leave raft building alone.

Suddenly out of the blue, one Saturday morning a few of the neighborhood boys met at my house and asked for my brother Charles. Talking excitedly, they started down the back alley with a saw and a hammer from our dad's tool box. I watched all this and felt left out of the group. Although I wasn't invited, I started to follow behind them, at a respectable distance, like a puppy dog. Down the alley, onto second Avenue they went. The group crossed the railroad tracks, past Girton Adams' Ice house, past Malloy's house on Second and Fifteenth, past the Yeager house on Thirteenth Street, past the gas house by the Tenth Street viaduct. Finally they were walking on the river wall that had been recently built to hold the river within its banks. This was an adventure within itself. The group got quieter now. No talking. They crossed the railroad bridge at the foot of Ninth Street, across from the Paint and Glass. Glancing in all directions and hoping that no one was around, the boys slowly crossed the last few ties of the bridge. All of a sudden a quick dash was made to get off the bridge and down the unwalled north bank of the river by Schoeneman Lumber. I still didn't have the foggiest notion of what was about to happen, but the big boys apparently did.

Down behind the willow trees along the bank, first one then another scooted over the wooden fence of the lumber yard. They started handing lumber, 2 X 4s, 1 X 8s, and 1 X 6s, through a hole in the fence. They knew what they needed and where it was.

The 2 X 4s were laid out in a pattern on a flat place on the bank. The flat pieces of lumber were laid down on top of the 2 X 4s after they had been nailed together. The flat pieces were then nailed to the 2 X 4s. Very little sawing was needed as the boys in the lumber yard had brought out lumber of equal length. All of this activity of placing the lumber on the ground and hammering took no more that a half hour. Everything was organized. The willow trees kept anyone from seeing what we were doing.

A raft had been made. We were Vikings.

*Diagram of a raft we built. (D.E. Fredricks)*

The Vikings were about to launch their boat. It was about five feet by six feet. The next step presented more of a problem than had been anticipated. It needed to be put into the river. As we attempted to slide it over the brush by the river and avoid falling into the river, the boat got hung up and wouldn't budge.

"Try again, now," one said determinedly. The raft was heavy and footing in the bush was difficult. Slowly and with great effort, it was pushed over the brush and it plopped into the river. A shout of joy went up, and quickly died when they realized they must keep quiet and not be detected by passerbys.

The raft floated in the water. "You get on it," one said. "Not me, I'm not crazy. Anyway I can't swim." Everyone looked around until Speed started toward the raft. The moment of decision. He looked at the raft, then lifted his legs to get on it. Everything looked great as he stepped on it. A moment, a long moment ticked while he stood there on the raft. Suddenly everyone began yelling and pointing at the raft. The raft began sinking. Speed's face began to show panic, but before he could jump off it and get back onto the bank, it stopped sinking. It stopped sinking at the level of Speed's ankles. It just didn't float, but then it didn't sink entirely either. He jumped off the boat. Then one of the other boys jumped onto the raft. Everyone was quiet again. They looked at the water up to the ankles of the boy. They all looked at each other dejectedly. No luck. *It wouldn't float with anybody on it...*

Poking it with a board like it was a dead animal didn't improve its floatability. Never the less we persisted in trying to ride it again, and again. After an hour of short excursions onto the river, keeping close to shore, we decided that it had been constructed wrong, but we didn't know how to correct it. After all, we were farm boys not sailors. It didn't go very far below the water, however, and that puzzled us. We thought it should go all the way to the bottom of the river.

We couldn't leave the raft by the lumber yard so it was decided that Veron would try to take it upstream and cross the river by floating it downstream, paddling to the other shore. It wasn't the best idea, as Vernon said, but it was the only one we could come up with. Two hours later it was resting on the south side of the river by the Tenth Street Viaduct. Branches were torn up and thrown onto the raft on the shore to camouflage it. That done, we all took off for home, as we were hungry. Supper was ready and a hard day's work had been done.

..............................

The railroad tracks again were our 'road' to the Drake Springs swimming pool. It was the shortest route to get there from where we lived on Third Avenue.

Out the front door, north down Third Avenue, a block to the railroad tracks which we then would follow to the railroad east. This was the easiest route. The adventure to get to the swimming pool on the East Side had begun.

It was a long walk for little legs so it had to be approached as if it was an adventure that would never come our way again. This took our minds off the actual distance we had to go. Challenges abounded and had to be overcome, some as great as what the pioneers had encountered on their journey to the West, we fantasized to ourselves.

The railroad tracks were considered the first great challenge of the trip. When you got to the tracks, and if you were athletic, (well what kid would admit that he wasn't?) the skill of balancing on the rails of the track had to be accomplished. God pray the tracks were not hot that day or too worn or too smooth with the passing of the trains. With arms extended for balance at our side like a big stork, the challenge was begun. The kids who could go the longest distance on the rails without falling off were the winners for the day. If you didn't compete, you were a rotten egg. Everyone tried it. The older kids, full of experience, usually had the knack of it down better than the younger ones, but the younger ones kept trying and falling off onto the ties and rock of the railroad bed, all of the time looking to make sure the train wasn't coming. Unless there was a path beside the tracks, the rails were easier to walk on than the rough, uneven rocks and creosote ties that held the rails in place. The creosote stunk and was miserable to get off of your bare feet. And you had to look out for the trains. What a thought, being squashed by a billion ton locomotive while walking on the rails. Life was fraught with danger. A lot of things had to be learned if you wanted to walk along the railroad tracks.

And sometimes a train came by.

As we stood alongside the train tracks, the exhilarating feeling of the passing train and the wind that the cars produced was beyond description.. It exhilarated and scared us at the same time. The attraction to the train was magnetic. It scared the hell out of us so much that sometimes we would fall to the ground to resist being sucked under the wheels or knocked over by an especially strong gust of wind. Or so it seemed. After the danger was over and the train had passed, we couldn't resist the thrill of rushing out onto the tracks and waving to the brakeman who stood in the caboose and waved back. Sometimes we had put a penny on the track before it had arrived and after we found the smashed coin, we marveled at the trains power to squash metal into weird, flat, unrecognizable forms. Its power was awesome.

The railroad was built here in the late 1870s along a small drainage creek that had to be filled in before laying the tracks, and then there were drainage ditches built along the tracks that collected the rain runoff from the streets. In the spring they were full of torrents of water but in summer, except after a rain, they were mostly dry enough so we could walk down them. Where the streets passed over the ditches, culverts went under the street to keep the water flowing and connect the ditches. Most of the culverts were only two feet in diameter except the one under Fourth Avenue. It was four feet in diameter...big enough for a kid to walk through it if he crouched down a little. Temptation comes in many forms and this challenge was too much temptation for the older, braver boys. The culvert presented a number of unique problems to those wanting to go through it. First, it wasn't straight. There was a slight curve half-way through it and this curve made it impossible to see the end of the long tunnel. The center was eerie and shrouded in darkness half-way through. Light travels in a straight line, but the tunnel didn't. The bottom of the culvert accumulated sand and debris making it difficult to walk on and sometimes pools of water accumulated in the sandy bottom of the culvert. Maybe alligators were in the water. You never know. You wanted to avoid these pools of water as you knew neither how deep they were or what was in them. The challenge to negotiate all of these barriers and still make it to the other end alive inflamed our hearts. Although no one was compelled to go through the culvert, you knew you were a man when you had gotten through it.

Or you could take the safe way and continue across Fourth Avenue on the railroad tracks and be safe from the dangers of life. But that was for sissies.

After crossing Fourth Avenue, the railroad tracks curved to the north where there were no trees. The hot sun beat down upon you unmercifully until the block passed and you reached Fourteenth Street. Fourteenth was a busy street. You had to be extra careful and watchful as you crossed it or you were road-kill material. After a mad dash across the street, we headed for the biggest cottonwood tree known in South Dakota at the time. It was on a triangular piece of land owned by Grandpa Robertson's, between the railroad tracks and Fifth Avenue. He wasn't our grandpa, but we called him that anyway. His tree was the biggest one we had ever seen. You felt compelled to feel the bark of the tree as you walked around it in wonder. How many houses could be built from it if it was chopped down? Millions? Or at least a half-dozen.

Continuing north on the tracks we passed the two-story Polar Cold Storage building on Thirteenth where the thought of their frozen ice cream pies in their freezer made my mouth water. I didn't understand how you could bake a ice cream pie without melting it. My neighbor who worked there assured me they did exist and she brought one home for me to try. It was heaven.

We were half way to the swimming pool, and only a block from the Big Sioux River. The smell of the dead fish in the river told us that.

Further north two railroad lines crossed, one going east and west, the other north and south. On Twelfth Street was a train roundhouse that was fascinating and fun for us to watch as the big train engines were being turned around on the giant turntable. There were three railroads that ran through or by the Gales Addition. The Chicago, St. Paul, Minneapolis, and Omaha Railroad cut a crescent shaped curve north east to north west through the old creek bed that we had just traveled. The Great Northern ran north-south just east and parallel to Eighth Avenue, and the Rock Island touched the northern boundary as it ran east and west to the downtown area of Tenth Street. The Rock Island had the roundtable built at the bottom of Fourth Avenue to turn their train engines around This created a curiosity area for the Galesburg region, as much activity was always occurring there. In fact there was some type of railroad activity somewhere around the Addition almost all of the time. We seemed to be confronted by its presence in almost every direction we walked. The sound of the train whistle never went unnoticed and its sound brought children as well as adults to attention. Effort was made to determine what way it was going and then if we could, we would run to a vantage point to watch its passing. Where it was going or coming from was always a constant question whenever we heard a whistle. Our limited, confined world couldn't fathom anything outside of our area. The "big world" was just a curiosity to us and we never ventured more than a few miles into it. The train whistle gave us some slight glimpse into a thought that someday we would get on one of the trains and see what that world was like.

In the '40s I had such a chance as I got on a steam engine in the dead of the winter and rode the steam train to Rowena. It was like being on a magic carpet.

Walking down the tracks was sometimes dangerous due to the increased train traffic and we usually turned east to walk down Thirteenth Street to cross the river at the Great Northern Bridge. We did, however, have a choice of two bridges for use in crossing the river. The Chicago, St. Paul, Minneapolis, and Omaha Railroad bridge was shorter but there was no way to get off it once we started across. This made us very anxious to move fast once we started across to avoid any train that might want to use it at the same time we did. The bridge had its support in the iron beams that were above the bed of the rails and ties. This was called a stress-supported bridge. Intriguingly, it had flat iron I-beams about a foot wide that supported the bridge and they had always looked inviting to climb on, but we never did. It was a thought, though.

The Great Northern bridge, to its east about three blocks about where Seventh Avenue would run through the area, was the preferred route to get across the river. It presented two ways to get across. There was no superstructure above the bed of rails and ties and there were spaces to the cement pillars that held the bridge up. If a train came along as you were crossing, you could climb down between the ties of the rails and wait while the train crossed over above you. Great fun! The huge cement footings used for supporting the skeleton of the bridge were wide platforms that offered a place to fish from. It was reached by shimming down between the ties of the rails like I just described to go fishing. Bullhead and carp fishing was good from these spots as you were out in the middle of the river where the water was deeper.

The other method of getting across the river at this point was by walking on top of a one to two-foot silver-painted natural gas pipe that had been suspended above the water and was supported by the bridge. This pipe originated at the natural gas storage tank on the south side of the river by Thirteenth Street. It crossed the river to transport gas to the East Side. The use of the pipe by the kids for crossing the river took a lot more skill than walking on the bridge. Again—another good challenge for the boys. The pipe was about two feet from the bridge structure and about ten feet above the water. If you stumbled or you lost your balance you ended up in the river, but this never happened to anyone I knew. It was tricky to do, but it was fun.

..............................

The Canaries, a professional baseball team in the 1930s, played their home field games at the Howard Wood Field on the East Side at Tenth and Franklin.

Athletic events were a welcome relief from the everyday humdrum activities. The Canary team players and other AAA teams had to struggle through life in the Heartland with the hope of "making it" in the big leagues, the likes of the New York Yankees or the Giants baseball teams.

Uncle Lawrence and his family lived near the Dairyland Creamery on Fairfax. Their home was on a high bluff that looked down on the baseball field a few blocks away. Home games were played at the Howard Wood Field on East Side. From this vantage point we could tell by the lights below when a night game was being played.

Numerous times I had seen the lights of the stadium while visiting my cousins and with apt curiosity watched the droves of people enter the stadium. Shouts of "oooos" and "aaaaahs" were heard periodically and then excited yells of ecstasy when the sound of a baseball being hit cracked from the stadium. Some of this activity could be seen from the hill, but most had to be imagined as the hedgefences around the stadium blocked out a lot of activity.

Neither my brothers nor I played baseball much. My parents never went to a Canary baseball game. I had played a little catch and a few makeshift baseball games in the street, but that was all. I was curious about what I saw from my uncle's house.

I was only eight or nine years old, but I had wanted to see what a real baseball game was like. I just had to see a game at least once.

By luck my parents and I visited my cousins on the night of a baseball game at the park. After lunch was over at Uncle Lawrence's the other kids went out to play, but I walked to the front porch overlooking the stadium a short distance below us. The lights were on and I knew that a game was to be played that night.

"Tonight I'm going to see a game," I vowed.

"O.K.," my Dad said, "but come back here after the game is over. We'll be here until 9:00 so be back by then." My heart was racing from the thought of going to the game. I left the front steps of the house, heading for the brightly lit stadium below.

I didn't know exactly how long a game would last and I had no watch to keep track of time, but that seemed to be a minor problem at the moment. I wanted to see a baseball game and nothing was going to stop me now. Opportunity had knocked and I was opening the door.

Talking with some of the neighbor boys, I had heard that there was a special way of getting into the stadium, but I wasn't sure how this worked. There was a group called the 'Knot Hole Gang' that could get kids in for free somehow. Nobody seemed to know how this worked, but the thought of going and seeing a baseball game kept festering in my mind; the thought would not go away. The only hope of seeing a baseball game was with the help of the "Knot Hole Gang," as my parents had no money to spend on such a frivolous event.

This term "Knot Hole" really intrigued me. I visualized people looking through a hole in the fence and seeing the game, but I knew that it must have been uncomfortable because I had heard that the games lasted for hours.

Confusion began to cloud my mind. People were hurrying everywhere. They seemed to know where they were going, but I didn't. Everything around me was confusing and unfamiliar. I thought it would be different somehow. Maybe I should go back home now and forget about the game.

Standing next to the curb and looking at the stadium I began regaining my composure. I stood back and watched for a while longer. People were going up to a little hole in the wall and getting pieces of paper from somebody I couldn't see. I heard a voice coming from the hole. All I saw was a hand coming out of the hole after the people gave some money to the person. Although I tried standing on my toes a number of times, I was still too short to see into the hole, but I kept watching the activity anyway. After getting a piece of paper, the people went through a gate and disappeared into the stadium. I looked through the gate as best I could and saw only the ends of seats and part of the field with players on it in the background.

Many minutes passed and I continued watching this activity before I tired of it and started walking toward the corner a few feet to the west. I looked down the dark side street that led from Tenth Street. Vaguely it looked familiar. Then it occurred to me that this side street went to the Girton-Adams River Ice Plant near the railroad and the Sioux River. The street was poorly lit and uninviting. Standing on the corner, I noticed that almost nobody was buying tickets anymore. The game had started as I heard a lot of yelling and screaming coming from inside the stadium.

Still looking down the side street, I finally noticed another gate about a half a block away. I began slowly walking toward it and peered in. An old man with a baseball cap on was standing at the gate with his back to the street and looking toward the baseball field. I couldn't see anything. My vision was blocked and all I could see were the ends of the bleachers with only a few people visible inside.

I felt completely alone. Why had I come? Maybe I should go home. Maybe it is time for Dad to leave for home. Oh, I wished I knew what time it was. My palms were sweating and I dried them on the side of my pants. I was getting more nervous now as I knew I had to be home by 9 o'clock. I didn't know what time it was.

'How would I get home if I missed my ride with my parents?' kept going through my mind.

I had come too far to turn back. I knew that I would have to persevere. Finally I got up the courage to walk up to the man at the gate who now kept looking at me.

In a cracking voice I asked "Where is the Knot Hole Gang?"

The man looked at him and broke into a grin.

"That way," the man pointed into the stadium,"go in and find a seat." Relief began to show on my face. Wow, that was easier than I thought it would be.

Not knowing what to expect, I slowly walked into the stadium and after glancing around getting my bearings, I sat down on the bleachers that were a short distance from a group of people in the stands. I looked around. There were quite few other kids sitting around me, but they were sitting with some adults who appeared to be in charge of them. I didn't recognize anybody. Could this be the Knot Hole Gang I had heard about? They were just kids like me.

Suddenly there was pandemonium as someone hit a home run.

"So this is the Knot Hole Gang," I said to myself. They weren't looking through any knot hole in the wood. Slowly it began to dawn on me that the Knot Hole Gang had nothing to do with knot holes in wood. I finally realized that it was only a saying pertaining to somebody who looks at a game for free. Now it was all clear to me. What a disappointment.

As the game progressed I began feeling nervous and panic set in. What time was it? I had become so engrossed in the activities at the stadium and it had taken me so long to get into the stadium that I kept feeling that it must be getting close to 9 o'clock. Maybe it is past nine o'clock.

The tension inside me became unbearable. Finally I couldn't stand it any longer. I decided he had to leave. I got up and headed for the exit. At the stadium gate I paused. Getting my bearings again I figured out that my house was somewhere south of here—on Third Avenue—which was about two miles the opposite way to my uncle's house on Fairfax. If I walked back to my uncle's house, I would be going away from my home on Third Avenue. Confused, I retraced my steps back to Tenth Street where I strained to see my dad's car in front of Uncle Lawrence's house. I crossed the highway on Tenth Street, heading north. Apprehension overtook me. This thought kept repeating itself in my head. If the car was gone, my parents would have already left for home and I would be left without a ride home. What was I to do if I missed his ride? My uncle didn't have a car so he wouldn't be able to take me home. What could I do? Panic. All of this was continuing to go through my mind again and again. What was I going to do? After crossing Tenth Street, the light from the stadium became less and less. After a long block of stumbling and walking and peering into the darkness to see my dad's car, I resigned myself to the fact that it was not parked in front the Uncle Lawrence's house. What to do now?

For some dumb reason known only to a kid, I suddenly turned around and began walking back toward Tenth Street. I decided that I was going walk to my Third Avenue home rather than go the rest of the way up the hill to my uncle's house.

Quickly I retraced my steps back to Tenth Street and headed west over the elevated viaduct that went over the many railroad tracks coming into Sioux Falls. The viaduct led to the Tenth Street bridge that went over the Sioux River.

After crossing the viaduct and the bridge, I turned south down Second Avenue toward home. I was getting scared now. It was dark on First Avenue. Dark and scary. Seven blocks later, at Seventeenth Street, I stood directly opposite my house that was on Third Avenue—but I was on Second Avenue. It was very quiet. Hauntingly quiet. There was nothing but darkness surrounding me. Only a vacant lot stood between me and home. I squinted to see if the lights were on at my house. They didn't appear to be on. "Damn it," I thought to myself, "nobody is home."

The street was dark as the only street light was many houses away and a feeling of panic about crossing the lot came over me. I had only recently seen a Frankenstein movie and the thought of monsters and eerie things crept over me. I was damned scared and I was getting more scared the more I gazed across the vacant lot. My mind said I should just start walking across the field but my feet didn't move my body. Finally the lack of valor got the best of me and I decided to walk the three extra blocks and stay on the sidewalk, where there was comfort in the streetlights. This was better than risking the chance of meeting Frankenstein in the alley by the house. Why had I seen that movie? I kept asking myself.

The extra three blocks were covered in record time. Home was only a few houses away. As I approached my house I noticed a car coming up the street. It was my parents. They had seen me turn back before getting to my uncle's house and figured that I had decided to walk home. "Why?" they asked. "Were you scared of the dark?" The car had been there in plain sight in front of my uncle's house. I just hadn't seen it.

*LIGHTS OUT, EV-RYBODY..........*

*Mom and brother Frank with the kittens. (FF Collection)*

*My sister, June, and her playthings. (FF Collection)*

*Winters were harsh on Third Avenue. (FF Collection)*

# 16

# The Big Dipper, Popcorn, Games, The Coat, Ice House

I was very mature for my age. When I was ten years old I took a part-time job at Loomis Grocery Store as a helper. The grocery store was to the north of Girton-Adams Ice Company on Second Avenue. The first chore I did for Mr. Loomis was to mow his extensive lawn. As I had a number of lawns that I regularly mowed, this was no big deal. The job inside the grocery store consisted of putting cans of food on the shelves, sweeping the floor, dipping up ice cream for cones, weighing out and sacking potatoes. I loved the task of sacking the potatoes. This task was done in the storeroom in the back of the store, behind the meat counter where Mr. Loomis spent most of his time. This way Mr. Loomis was close by to check up on me at first, but as he found me to be competent at this chore, he grew to trust me and he left me alone. This task gave me time to sit and think as I weighed out correct amounts of potatoes for each sack. It also gave me a chance to be alone for a long time and use some of the mathematical skills I had learned in Longfellow School. That really gave me confidence. From the meat counter in the back of the store Mr. Loomis could advise and supervise the two women clerks who took care of the cash register and other duties in the front of the store. It was a great observation point behind the meat counter, as he could view the entire store and also step back into the storeroom for special orders of customers.

Another duty that I enjoyed was dipping ice cream. For a nickel one could get two large scoops of either vanilla, chocolate, cherry, butterscotch, or strawberry ice cream, for the single-cake cone. You had a choice: you could get the same type or any combination dipped into the cone—in generous proportions.

On one of the days that I was not needed at the store, I decided to go to a movie at the Grenada Theater at Eighth and Phillips Avenue. The Grenada had the best deal in town for movies as there were always double-feature movies with a half hour of advertisements shown in between. As it was a twenty to thirty minute walk to the theater if you procrastinated, I decided to get a ice cream cone to eat on the way.

One of the perks of working at a grocery store was that I could dip my own cone. With the dipper in my right hand, I dipped into the vanilla. That dip looked delicious, so I put another on top of it to complete the double dip for the nickel. Man it looked good! My mouth began watering. The chocolate ice cream caught my eye. That looked good too. Without thinking, I immediately put a dip on top of the vanilla. Wild. My head began reeling. That dip was followed by another dip of the same kind to complete the double dip again. By this time my mouth was salivating like a Pavlov dog and I felt myself a little out of control. The dipper didn't want to stop. It had a mind of its own. A dip of cherry ice cream went on top of the chocolate followed by butterscotch. Reality overtook me. God, what have I done? I looked at the six scoops of ice cream and became frightened. Enough, I thought. I glanced up from the ice cream containers and caught a glimpse of Mr. Loomis and a clerk. They both were watching me and they had wide smiles on their usually glum faces. Sheepishly I looked back at the cone but I knew it was too late to put any of the ice cream back. I quickly put the scooper down, walked to the counter by the cash register and left a dime and a nickel.

The day was warm but not hot. The ice cream began to slowly melt. Quickly I licked at the drips. They were coming faster. I had to keep rotating the cone and licking like mad to keep the melting ice cream from dripping onto the ground. It was a struggle, but I kept up with it. Street after street I kept licking, checking the entire cone for drips and watching the curbs so that I wouldn't stumble as I crossed the intersections. I arrived at the theater with the cone well under control, but it was getting the best of me. It was a lot of ice cream and I was getting full. In the cool theater the cone lasted through almost the first feature before I finished it....and boy, was I sick of ice cream. I never created a cone that big again although I was often tempted to.

..............................

There is nothing as good in life as a handful of popcorn, unless it is a sack of popcorn. God outdid himself when he created popcorn.

Those delectable little white, popped kernels afford a mouth-watering delectable snack that can almost make you feel like killing for. Each kernel individually or an entire handful can be popped into your mouth to satisfy the taste buds. It can be eaten "dry", with a touch of butter, or smothered in butter. I prefer a touch of butter; one of my sisters likes a lot of butter, and if she pops it, that's how we eat it; my other sister pops it with no butter on it. To each his own.

When Lewis Drug Store opened on Phillips Avenue in the early 1940s, the first attraction that was inside the doors was a large, beautifully-lit popcorn popper. It stood there like a beacon beckoning the customers off of the street. It was extremely hard to resist. Anybody who approached the popper was met by an aproned clerk that appeared out of nowhere. If there hadn't been a sack of corn prepared beforehand, a large metal scooper was shoved into the corn as a sack was "popped" open with a sharp downward thrust of the other hand, and before you knew it, a tall—foot tall—sack of popcorn was thrust into your hand and five cents was collected from you. The sack of popcorn was monstrous. It appeared almost as large as some of the kids that carried them. You could eat for hours out of it before you either got full or it was gone. There was enough in it for two or three members of the family—unless you were a kid, then there was never enough. All of this for a nickel.

On trips downtown, the aroma of the corn popping could be smelled a block away. As one approached the store, the popping sound was music to the ears. Lines formed as it popped not only to get the corn but to savor the experience of it being popped. Watching the corn pop was almost as good as going to a movie. Almost.

The only better feeling was getting a bag of popcorn and going to a triple movie at the Grenada Theater. We wanted to buy the huge sack of corn at Lewis Drug because it was twice as much as you got at the movie house. Every time I bought popcorn at Lewis on the way to the movie, however, I became very apprehensive. My concern was that the people at the movie wouldn't let me carry my Lewis corn into the theater. Would I have to throw the corn away or simply put the movie on hold until I ate all of it? This type of dilemma created many sleepless nights for me. What would you have done?

..............................

Although it was probably an oversight by the planning commission of the city, Seventeenth Street was omitted from Phillips east to Seventh Avenue which produced an excessively long, nice quiet nonintersection street from Fourteenth to Eighteenth on Third Avenue. This four-block-long, paved street was especially good for the kids in the winter time when the city would block the intersections of Eighteenth and Nineteenth Street and allow the kids to sled on the snow from Nineteenth Street all the way to Fifteenth Avenue. For those older kids that could manipulate their sleds the right way, this five block ride was quite exhilarating after the snow in the still of the cold winter nights. The numerous children that would congregate after supper had the best carefree time of their lives yelling and screaming to their hearts' delight as numerous of sledders would do a number of runs down the hill until the cold necessitated a return trip to their home to get warmed up. The return trip back up the hill in heavy winter gloves and snow suits gave everyone ample time to discuss their skills in sledding or banter back and forth about each other's day at school. The thrill of the ride down the hill was unbelievable and more than compensated for the long walk back hauling the heavy sleds. It was almost as much fun as the anticipation as putting your wet tongue on the iron of the sleds.

.................................

The winters were cold in Sioux Falls. Temperatures of below zero were the norm after December, and it took a good coat to shield you from the intense wind and cold.

The depression put holes into the job market and good, hard-working people fell through them. Jobs were scarce and the ones that were still there paid very little money. A family such as ours, with eight children, a mother and father—ten in all—had to be very frugal in order to make the twenty dollars a week last for everything. Food was adequate, if not abundant, and a garden in the back yard supplemented the fare on the table. Furniture was kept until it no longer was usable, and then the wood was burned in the cookstove.

Clothes were another thing. A family couldn't raise sheep in the city for wool. No longer did anyone but farmers raise cattle for the leather products they could furnish. Our mother did what most mothers in the 30s did, she sewed what clothes she could to supplement the needs of the family. She used a Singer sewing machine, a treadle machine that needed her foot power. I remember how she spent many hours at the machine. Sometimes she moved the machine next to a window for the best light during the day. The hum of the Singer sewing machine was comforting to us because we knew at some point she would look up from the machine and tell one of us to "try this on". After a few minor adjustments to the clothing, we would then be the proud possessor of a new shirt, mended pants, or whatever. It would be the last new thing we would get until we had a birthday, when the present usually consisted of clothes. A new item of clothing could lift a kid's spirit right up out of the depression.

I dreamed of having a new coat. Not a coat handed down to me from my brothers, or in some instances even from my older sisters. I remember, when I was very young, getting my sister's coat when she was through with it. It had a few good wears left in it, so I wore it. But I wanted a *new* coat.

We often had get-togethers with our numerous cousins at our house on Third Avenue. We never went to a McDonalds or Burger King in the 30s. They didn't exist, and, even if they had existed, we could not have afforded them. After one of our get-togethers for a family birthday party celebration, I discovered a sheepskin jacket left on one of the chairs. It was the most beautiful coat I had ever seen. It had rough brown leather on the outside and soft white wool on the inside. I picked it up. It was heavy. Sheep wool is heavy, I thought to myself. Whose could it be? I tried it on. It fit. Well, it almost fit. It fit good enough to have been mine. But it wasn't mine, I reminded myself. Whose could it be? I tried to remember all who had been at the party. The only one I could think of who might own it was my cousin, Homer. He was older than me, but I was large for my age. It must be his. I asked my mother if it was his. Probably it was, she said. "We'll have to give it back to him the next time he comes here," she said. The next time. That could be months. All through the night the wind prowled outside and tried to get in. It was winter and it was cold. The sheepskin coat was beautiful. I couldn't get it out of my mine. I dreamed about it that night. It was warm. It was mine. I saw myself wearing it everywhere. Everybody was amazed that I had such a beautiful coat.

After getting up early the next morning and eating a quick breakfast, I put on the coat and walked to Longfellow School. It was a windy, blustery cold winter day with flurries of snow. I didn't care. I had a sheepskin coat. After entering the school grounds, I walked out into the middle of the large playing field to the east of the school, and just stood there. It was a great feeling. "Here I am," I said to myself, "with my cousin's coat on, and I can stand out in the middle of the schoolyard and be warm." I stood there for a long time in the cold, in the wind, with the snow blowing around me. Finally I went into the warmth of the school building. The next day my cousin returned and picked up *my* sheepskin coat.

Years later, in warm and sunny California, my wife and kids bought me a sheepskin coat. Once or twice a year, during the coldest weather, I will go down to his basement, turn off the heat and watch TV for an hour or two with my sheepskin coat on, reliving the schoolyard memory. Somehow...it's not the same.

...............................

The lack of through-traffic on Third Avenue encouraged the kids to use the paved road in front of our house, in summer as well as in winter.

Across the street under the single dim street light that hung from a light pole, was where the hours-long games of hide-and-seek or kick-the-can would originate in the short summer nights. The longer nights of spring or fall afforded more time for play before the ten o'clock curfew stopped all play. In the summers the wait for darkness produced many variations of games such as 'Statue of Liberty' while waiting for darkness to come.

Kick-the-can or hide-and-seek were the favorites of the neighborhood kids. Any number of kids at any age could participate and the mind went wild at the thought of finding a place to hide that would stump the seeker. It was a lonely job being the seeker if there developed a conspiracy among the hiders to fool the seeker and go home after a while leaving the seeker

*My children answered my wish for a new sheepskin coat. (FF Collection)*

high and dry looking for non-existent players. Usually after a while of no luck at finding hiders, the seeker got the message and announced to the street-light that he was going home also.

................................

A once important ritual that has faded from the American scene is the trip to the ice house. The invention and perfection of modern refrigeration has decreased the ice houses' importance in the community. This was not the case in the '30s and '40s, however.

The icebox had been invented to utilize the principle that cold temperatures slowed the spoilage of food, and made drinks taste better. Every house, even the humblest, boasted an icebox in which to put ice during the summer. It was a simple device, an insulated box with a door with the ice being placed in a top compartment so the cooler air could drift downward and cool the food inside.

The demand for ice was determined by the temperature of the Heartland summer. On hot days it melted faster and on cool days it lasted longer. The hottest weather was dreaded the most as the ice seemed to melt almost overnight. These were the times that a trip to the icehouse was needed to replenish the ice supply. The trip became a ritual that the kids looked forward to. There was a pair of ice tongs hanging on the back shed wall that needed to be put in the car. The monstrous jaws of the ice tongs appeared to be a ferocious jaw of a shark and we loved to play like we were monsters when we took them to the car.

I once had to go to the icehouse for ice on my bicycle while living on Third Avenue. It was over three blocks away from home and I made it there easily by way of the back alley. I could not use the alley for the return trip, though, as it was not paved or smooth enough to keep the ice in the bike's basket. Also I could put only a 25-pound block in the basket on my bike, and that was very precarious. The trip home was a nightmare that I remember vividly. It was impossible to steer the bicycle with the huge block of ice in the front basket and I kept running off the sidewalk. My greatest fear of dropping the block of ice did not happen, but the constant pressure of keeping it in the basket completely exhausted me by the time I got home.

The use of a bicycle was not the usual method of getting the ice blocks home. In order to transport the ice blocks home, the front bumper of dad's car was used. The ice block was placed on it, careful to have it leaning back toward the car, and rechecked to make sure it wouldn't move. If it was hot outside, only a few minutes were needed for it to melt a little onto the metal bumper and become very secure. The road between First and Second Avenues was a nightmare. It was extremely bumpy. Rough roads and bumps had to be taken slowly in order to keep the ice on the bumper or it would flip off and shatter into a hundred pieces. Slow and with caution was the watchword while Dad drove the return trip home.

Arriving home, Dad immediately used the tongs to lift the 50-pound ice block into the top door of the ice-box and we were ready for another day of blistering heat, secure in our knowledge that our food would not spoil.

*Meet me in St. Louis, Louie, Meet me at the fair..........*

Frances Stockinger • Paul Stockwell • Charles Stoneback • Pat Strain • Bill Stringham • Virginia Stanton Stuerman • Margaret Berrett Ed Sunderman • Dick Swedeen • Joan Tabor • Gerald Teslow • Carol Ther • Hazel Thesenvitz • Beverly Thomas • Leonard Thomas • Charles Thurston • Les Tiezen • Daisy Christopulos Till • Bill Townley • Avis Druger Tracy • Harold Harry Marv Donald Tunge• John Turner • Betty Hoefert Twedt • Norma Main Donna Reit Cora Williams James Tyler • Jim Unzicker • Nickerson Donna Thomas Janice Haas Verta • Tom Vick • Loretta Joe Vosika • Robert Walker • Bonnie French Wallenstein • Jim Walter • Bob Wagner • Bob Karen Walton • Gerald Warren • Hattie Warren • Dwane Watson • Rodney Watson • Morton Weiss • Marie Welliever • Joyce West • Jim Norm Westby • Lila Lee Whaley • Lloyd Richard Whaley • Leora Ostrosky Whaley • Dolores Whitcomb • Murray Widdis • Marie Bingen Gary John Wilcox • Paul Willadson • Carl Walt Wilson • Cora Tyler Williams • John Winebag • John Winters • Dick Wold • Darlene Davis Woods • Dennis Wright • Jim Wylie • Andrew Katherine Bert Florence Isabel Ruth John Chapman Douglas Beth Rober Bert Donald Lawrence Yaeger • Andrew Louisa Andrew Katherine Harry Calla May Hiram Grow Lila Frank Bert Grow Yeager • Marilyn Youngren • Bill Zaayer • Barbara Zimmerman • Bill Ziske • Lillian Aaland • Evelyn Amdahl • Ruth Bach • Ethyle Barry • Clara Beardsley • Effie Benson • Helen Bliss • Boyd Bohlke • Eadess Brekke • Ada Brown • Lucille Bruce • William Bubbers • Glen Bunday • Robert Burns • Elizabeth Caldwell • Iline Carlton • Robert Chaussee • Clark Close • Marie Conway • Helen Dahl • Wally Diehl • Lynn Engen • Doug Evens • Robert Evens • Marjorie Evenson • Frances Farley • Almelyne Flint • Frances Flint • Helen Frease • Faye Frick• Dorothy Furrow • D. Goldsmith • William Graves • Joy Hamrin • William Hand • Elmer Hansen • Chester Hauge • Grant Heckenlively • Paul Heide • Harold Hoover • Paul Hutton • Borghild Johnson • Muriel Jones • Donald Jorgensen • Andrew Kleinsasser • Fred Kohoutek • Lester Kremer • Terine Kron • Lillie Kunkle • Joseph Lemohn • Arnold Lowe • Helen McQuillen • Emma Miller • Geraldine Molseed • Noel Muller • Arthur Nelson • Hannah Nordgren • Lorraine Norman • Muriel Nuffer • Clara Ollenburg • Irene Olson • Birde Posthuma • Ferdinand Rayl • Dorothea Riter • Helen Ronan • Ben Rossow • Felix Schwartz • Charles Sidlo • Ellen Skaff • Eudora Stegner • Leonard Tabor • Arthur Thompson • Homer Thurston • Josephine Wagner • Fidelis Walter • Gertrude Weeldreyer • Helen Whitman • Alphus Wilson • Ashton Wilson • Joyce Feay • Melvern Metcalf

# 17
# World War II

The '30s was a period of little growth in the population of South Dakota.

Actually, there was a great exodus out of the state during the depression, especially by the young people. The Sioux Valley, however, didn't change greatly due to its unique situation. For every person that left the Sioux area to seek his fortune in another state, there was a replacement for him from the outlying towns. There always seemed to be hope for more work in the bigger cities like Sioux Falls than in the small towns. This has been the flow of population in the l900s and the cities had in the past absorbed this hope. But when the unique industrial needs of the '30s was halted by the depression, the population only accumulated and stagnated in the cities that had offered them so much hope. This concentration only helped the welfare system distribute its aid easier. The social agencies were more organized and they didn't carry the social stigma like they did in the small towns.

World War II changed everything in the 1940s.

A sudden patriotism erupted and the enthusiasm of enlisting in the Army overtook farm and city boys alike. The trains heading out of Sioux Falls toward Kansas and Illinois were filled with the young draftees that were needed to fight oppression in Europe and Asia.

Suddenly the Government announced that an Army Radio Training School was to be built on l,500 acres of land near the airport between West Sioux Falls and Covell Lake. Everyone became excited with the prospect of a great deal of activity and full employment in the area again. The opportunity to make money made the businessmen's heads giddy. Prosperity would surely return. JOBS.......JOBS.......JOBS........ Six-hundred barracks were needed for the radio school. Five thousand workers were needed. Right now. Five-thousand workers! Full employment after ten years of loss of hope during the depression. The search to get these thousands of carpenters, truck drivers, plumbers, ditch diggers, and machine operators necessary to build the five to six-hundred barracks needed for the radio school began. Five-thousand workers had to be rounded up to do the job in the day and night, five-month schedule allotted. The logistics to complete this were mind-boggling.

Newspapers all over South Dakota, Minnesota, and Iowa carried the message of need. There were no young people to fill the needs; they were going off to war but the older workers came by the droves. The city was overwhelmed with new people. They needed to live and sleep someplace. But where? Any space that could be used as a sleeping room was rented sight-unseen. The buses ran full and the bars hummed with business night and day. Full employment and the better times had returned to the Heartland.

Rent control quickly followed along with the rationing of the necessities of life. Along with all of this prosperity came the opportunists of gain. Their appetite had to be controlled.

The Second World War was a time of great hardship and sacrifice for everyone. It was expected. The 'boys' were off to war, and the community supported them. Whole-heartedly they supported them. The sacrifice on the 'homefront' was to be expected, and given. Gasoline, sugar, canned goods, meat, and shoes were rationed. Ration coupons were needed to purchase these items. Victory gardens were started on every available empty lot in the city and the surplus was canned for the winter. Corn syrup was substituted for granular sugar, which was nearly impossible to get. If you knew a farmer that could get you meat, you were considered very fortunate.

Scrap metal was needed to make steel to fight the "Japs" and "Huns." A scrap-metal site was designated on the empty lot to the east of the Arkota ballroom building. Scrap drives were organized. The patriotic citizens of the city collected the scrap metal in their houses and garages and gave it to help the war effort. Everyone must sacrifice. The pile grew to immense proportions until it was taken away on the trains to be used in making steel for the tanks and other equipment for the war. Tires were rationed. No more would be available for the general public until the war was over. The tires on cars were babied until they could not be used any more and then they were collected to be remade into new tires for jeeps. Gasoline was rationed. Coupons were needed to buy gasoline. 'A', 'B' and 'C' gasoline ration stickers became prevalent on all of the windshields of the cars. The entire Heartland was geared to win the fight for democracy.

The tar-sided Army base barracks were hastily put up on cement foundations and the soldiers began arriving by the same trains that had taken the recruits out of town. Troop trains lined up by the Milwaukee depot at the north of Phillips Avenue became a common site for the duration of the war.

The city was bursting at the seams with soldiers. Soldiers were everywhere one turned. They strolled the streets, they filled the bars, they crowded the swimming pools until it became imperative that they had to build their own recreation facilities at the air base. Hotels were filled with their wives on their too-short visits and the wives that wanted to stay would live in almost any space a bed could be put. War bond drives to finance the war were started. All the school kids saved their money and bought stamps at school for ten cents each. After accumulating enough to fill their little books they turned them in for a real U.S. Government war bond.

................................

World War II demand for many materials created a drought of toys for kids. Metal wagons and tricycles could not be bought at any price for the duration of the war. The metal was needed to build tanks to fight the enemy "huns" and the "Japs".

The war, however, created a climate that fostered a great deal of imagination.

My buddy Dick was a doodler. I picked up the habit and eventually got very good at it, too. My imagination ran wild whenever I picked up my pencil and began to draw. The drawings we made was a good mental activity that kept us out of trouble. Having been fortunate enough to have a buddy like Dick, I learned to diagram various plans of airplanes, ships, tanks, and cars. I was good at this type of 'doodling'. A war was on. The government needed our help in inventing new weapons to help win the war. Or so we thought.

The war touched everything. Even the comic books. One of the popular comic books, Captain Midnight, encouraged youngsters to send in "inventions" and drawings done by the reader. Perfect. I sent in many drawings over a period of months and then anxiously waited for a return confirmation notice of acceptance from the publisher. I did receive two or three certificates from the publisher and I faithfully bought the comic book each month with my hard earned ten cents, but I never saw any of my "inventions" in the book. Eventually I realized that I would never be discovered and given appropriate reward for my pastime.

It was during the summer of 1943 that I began putting my talent of diagramming to a real test. I needed something to do and I, being influenced by the war that was raging, decided to build a 'tank' out of wood. Wood from discarded shipping crates that my father had brought home from the Paint and Glass Company was selectively gathered from a pile in the back yard. Nails were pulled out of the boards and inspected for soundness. I saved the nails. Both nails and good straight wood would need to be used for the project. The boards were then separated for length and size. Decisions had to be made for the different types of wood needed—2X 4s for the frame,—1 X 6s and 1 X 8s for the siding and roof. Plans were carefully drawn for the four-foot side walls. Tanks had to have a place for the guns on the top. A turret on the roof. Make it square? Real tanks were round, but it would be too difficult to make it round. Square. OK. The tank was to be narrow enough to be run down the sidewalk but big enough for me to get inside and steer it. I measured the width of the sidewalk in front of my house. Plans were checked and rechecked with modifications made for added portholes in the turret. I needed to be able to look out so I could see where I was going.

With hammer and saw in hand, I began construction; slowly and deliberately, measuring and remeasuring to be sure. Nailing the boards together was easy for me. The saw presented somewhat of a challenge. Tough to get a straight cut, but they would do. Lay out the boards, look them over, then decide what to do. Nail now? OK. After the floor boards had been nailed down and the shell of the 2 X 4s in place for the sides, a soldier from the Army Air Base appeared suddenly in the backyard as I was working. The soldier had been strolling past the house when he saw me busily working. He had become curious and decided to check my project. "Nice job, kid," he said. "Here, let me check it out." After a thorough examination of the completed work and my plans, he nodded approval and held a board as I nailed it to the side. "Good job, keep it up. Got to go. Need to get back to the base."

It got dark. I had worked throughout the afternoon without stopping. I slept well that night.

It took another morning to complete the sides and the top turret of the tank. When completed, the inside was large enough to sit with my feet stretched out before me. The top slots in the turret were great, they afforded the vision I needed to see out. I had to crouch on my knees to get my head into the turret. I put moveable boards on nails so that the slits could be closed. What a tank. Just like a real one. It was comfortable inside. And secure. The frame and sides were complete. Looking at it for a while, I walked over to the tank and tipped it over on its side. I finally pushed until it sat on its top. Upside down. Wheels were needed to move it and I figured out a way to put them on. A 2 X 4 wider than the tank was bolted onto the bottom front center of the tank and a pair of salvaged buggy wheels were nailed to the back of the frame and it should run now. It took another hour of grunting and groaning to upright the monstrosity. A piece of rope was found and hooked to the front 2 X 4 to provide steering of the wheels. The rope was then run into the tank through a hole so I cold pull on it and steer from inside.

Now I was ready for the road test.

All of a sudden it dawned on me. I couldn't push it, steer it, and ride inside at the same time. I was devastated at my ignorance. After numerous attempts to move it, I discovered that it was too large and too heavy for me alone. I gave up and rested for a while. Help was obviously needed. Speed, Roger, Bill, Dean and a couple of other boys from the neighborhood had to be recruited to get to the front sidewalk. Then I found out that the tank body was narrow enough for the sidewalk, but the 2 X 4 that held the front

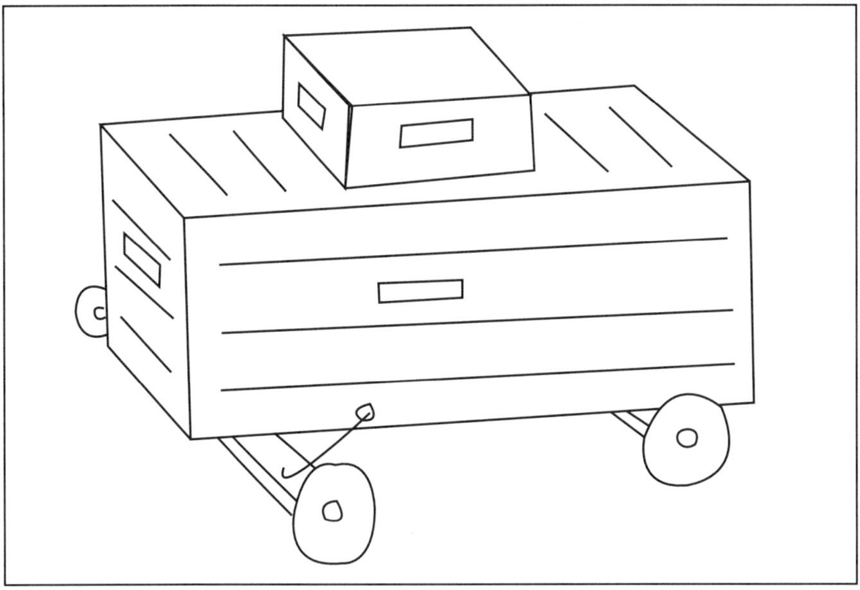

*Tank Diagram. (FF Collection)*

wheels was wider than the sidewalk. The front wheels rode on the grass while the rear wheels rode on the sidewalk.

PUSH....PUSH I yelled out to my buddies outside of the tank.

Slowly it moved. It moved with difficulty but it moved. As it was down hill it picked up speed as it was being pushed by the boys. Then I felt a loud 'CRUNCH'. The tank stopped. What now? I got out of the tank door in the rear and then realized that the wide wheels had collapsed under the weight of the tank. It took me ten minutes to fix the wheels and by that time my 'slaves' had gotten bored and left. I was now left to fend for myself. After having worked all day on the tank, I was tired and thirsty. My cousin lived nearby so I decided to go get a drink of water and rest a spell to decide my next moves. As I started walking into the front door of his house, I heard a loud noise that sounded like a car hitting a tree. As I turned quickly around I heard voices saying, "Let's get out of here." Two big older boys from Fourth Avenue had tipped over the tank and were running away from it. Man, was I steamed. It really bugged me that those big bullies would do something like that. But they never did get along with the kids on Third Avenue. It took me a number of minutes to get over my anger and then I started trying to upright it. A couple of kids came by and helped me. Luckily the tank wasn't damaged and the kids helped me push it back up the street to my home. After struggling to get it into the back yard, I just stood there and looked hopelessly at it. It didn't take long to realize that it was too big to be used as intended.

What to do with it?

I'll use it as my clubhouse! Yes, that's it. It was big enough. I put a hinged door with a lock on it and I bought some candles at the store. I collected all of my comic books from the house and put them inside. The candles provided my light and the comic books provided my entertainment.

Over the next year many hours were spent in contemplation and reading in this makeshift clubhouse. It was my refuge from the family and the neighborhood. Snacks were kept in it and I slept out in it a number of times. Occasionally in the winter I would buy a quart of chocolate milk and I would keep it in the clubhouse for only myself. That was a luxury that I wanted only for myself. Paper and pencils were kept in there and I would idle away hours doodling.

Years later when my family moved to Fifteenth and Elmwood, the wooden tank took four people to move it onto the bed of the movers truck.

Don't sit under the apple tree with anyone else but me..........

# 18
# Life on the farm

City life is great, but a farm is heaven, especially to a nine-year old.

In the spring of 1943, Ed Entrim bought an eighty-acre farm a mile to the east of Rowena. The farmer who was there before Ed had let the hog shed and a few other buildings fall into disrepair. They had to be rebuilt.

The idea of being on a farm really excited me. Visions of riding horses, plowing fields for planting, running wild and free crossed my mind. While on the farm I felt completely independent, free. I was my own man. A whole new part of the world was about to be opened to me, and explored. The first thrill came in just getting to the farm. It was especially fun riding in the Model T truck as Ed drove to Rowena. This trip down the old two-lane Highway 38 toward Iowa seemed like a trip to the end of the world.

Ed was a carpenter and I had met him while he was building a house on Second Avenue. He had built a number of houses on Second Avenue and Eighteenth Street, as well as his son's house at Twenty-third and Ninth Avenue. After hanging around and watching the construction men building a house on Second Avenue, Ed had asked me if I wanted a job cleaning the wood out of the yard around the building? "Sure." I replied. It wasn't much of a job but I liked being around the job site and watching the carpenters work. They treated me like a man and this made me feel good. The job didn't last long enough and before long Ed had another project. A farm.

The coming of the Second World War put a halt to home construction. Lumber was put on a priority list and almost all of it was used for Government construction. Ed had to find other ways to get the lumber he needed to rebuild the farm he now had. Suddenly the opportunity appeared. Army barracks were to be built on a site near West Sioux Falls and the Lakeside Dairy barns that stood on the site by Burnside Street had to be torn down. The wood was to be salvaged and taken to a farm near Rowena. It was a rush job to tear down the dairy barn and we worked like hell alongside a number of other carpenters who was salvaging the lumber also.

With the diligence that only a Midwesterner can muster, Ed soon had the repair job on the farm under way and the hog shed was quickly repaired. Repair on the chickencoop was the next project. After that was repaired, a new, two-car garage was built, as there was no garage on the farm. The activity exhilarated me. I would like to think that I was a big help in rebuilding the farm, but as I was only nine years old, my help was limited. Most of my time at the farm was spent exploring the farm where there was continual adventure. Ed didn't live on the farm while this construction was going on, but rather he lived in his duplex on Eighteenth Street. Because of this, I had to be at his house early in the morning in order to ride out to the farm with him. Many times I did not get to his house in time and Ed refused to wait for a kid that may never show up, so he left without me. When this happened I hitch-hiked to Rowena.

I enjoyed working at carpentry, and I loved working with Ed. He became like a father to me. I enjoyed the individual attention that only a single child in a family can get. Ed and his wife,Bessie, had a son and daughter-in-law that they loved but I was like a 'new' grandchild and they doted on me.

There was so much for a nine-year-old to explore and to learn on a farm. It was a great adventure just learning what the numerous buildings on the farm were used for. First off was the barn. It was too big to hide and it attracted the greatest curiosity. The barn, two stories of wood and nails, with great gaping holes to put things into and take things out of, intrigued me. Early in the morning and in the afternoon cows were milked here. Hay stored in the loft for the winter. Hay or straw? What's the difference? One or the other was stored there. The dark, mysterious hole where we shoved hay (or straw) down to the animals on the first floor scared me to death.

I found out that the chickens liked to lay their eggs in the hay loft. The chickens were very secretive and inventive about the whereabouts of their nests. I felt like a detective when I had to gather the eggs for Bessie in the evening. If you didn't find the nest, the eggs could rot, and what we did with the rotten eggs is a completely different story. The hayloft was used for play when kids from other farms came around to visit. We would swing on the ropes from side to side, then let go of the rope, and alight in the deep hay unhurt. Great fun.

The hog shed was a long building with the pens along the sides and a center area for walking. On each side of the center isle were the pens where the pigs were kept. The mother and father pigs were huge. And odd looking. The little pigs were cute to watch, but their mothers and fathers could be quite mean. You had to continually watch out for the adults because they would take a bite that could be quite painful. When I first went to the farm, I wondered where their mouths were. All I ever saw the pigs do was put their noses down in the mud and 'rut' the ground. I never saw their mouths, so I thought they got their food through their noses. Much later I discovered that there was a mouth, with teeth, under that strange nose.

The chickens had a house of their own. The chickencoop. It was smaller than the other farm buildings. At night the chickens slept in the coop. During the day, they roamed freely around the farm and found seeds and whatever to peck at. Feeding them was an event in itself. When Bessie emerged out of a shed with a bucket of corn, chickens would converge from every direction of the large yard. They would come running from everywhere, hell bent for leather, trying to be first and get the most feed. It was always quite a spectacle.

Chicken dinners were never a time of happiness for me. I was never very fond of the method of getting the chickens that Bessie used when they were going to have chicken for dinner. I watched in awe and horror at what she did to the chicken before she plucked the feathers off of them. They had to be killed! Some farmers wrung the necks of the chickens, but Bessie cut their heads off with a hatchet. Having to cut off their heads when we wanted to eat one was not a humane way of killing a chicken, I thought. This experience was like having a cold bucket of water thrown in your face on a hot day. It was a shock to me, a shock that took a long time to get over.

The thought of going to the farm excited me every time I was asked to go there. I loved being on the farm, out in the country, far away from the big city.

"I have to go over to the neighbors," Ed said one day. "Come on, you can drive."

"Drive? Drive what? What do you mean?" I asked astonishedly.

Ed walked out of the house and I followed. We crossed the yard, closed the gate, and he kept walking toward the barn.

"The car is over there," I said to Ed. "We passed the garage."

Ed kept walking. We reached the shed and he swung open the doors. There stood the tractor. The big, green-painted John Deere, just like the ones across from the County Courthouse in town. We loved going to get milk at Walt and Mary's dairy store in the evening. As we sat waiting for Dad or Mom while they got the milk buckets filled, we could look at the big outdoor sign of a deer on the John Deere building.

Ed got up on the tractor, started it, and backed it out of the shed. "Okay, get up here," he gently commanded. "It's time you learned to drive the John Deere tractor." I looked up at Ed. I had never driven a car, let alone a tractor. I had ridden in the car many times and pretended to drive it, but I had never actually driven it. I had watched as Ed shifted gears, pulled levers, and turned the steering wheel. I'm only nine years old! I can't even drive a car, but I climbed up. It was scary. Ed held me on his lap as he showed me what the levers and pedals were used for. I picked up the knack fast. At first Ed directed my hand to the levers but shortly I began doing adjustments of the gas lever myself. Within a short time I was driving the huge machine down the road by myself. At least I felt I was doing everything myself. What a feeling of power. At nine years of age this was a tremendous accomplishment. What a thrill.

This was the start of another phase of farming. I became more helpful and took command when Ed needed me. There were many small chores that I was capable of doing now, like driving the large green, John Deere tractor when I had to pull the wood sled with the water barrels on. That was the first time I had driven the John Deere to the pasture for the sleds to take water to Ed's cows. I was only nine years old, but felt like twenty. Later that summer I had my first experience driving the Model-A truck, in a corn field where there was nothing to hit. This required much more skill and coordination than driving the tractor. The ploughed corn field was extremely rough and the two of us bounced up and down almost hitting the roof of the cab. Somehow or other this rough treatment caused a flat tire that we had to repair.

I really enjoyed being a farmer.

..............................

Farm life requires a person who can tolerate being alone for many hours in the week. Sometimes this means many lonely hours at a time as duties are performed in remote sections of the farm. The pressure of deciding when to plan the crops, when to harvest the crops, and constant everyday decisions relating to running the farm make for a lonely, and independent life for the farmer. You must acquire this type of personality or perish in the farming business.

But all was not bleak. Quiet and isolation was what I liked. It was what I craved many times. I had become somewhat of a loner and I needed quiet time to think about things other people took for granted. I liked looking at the hills on the farm, I liked watching the corn grow. I enjoyed milking the cow. Well...most of the time.

There was one event that occurred on the farm that became a routine and I looked forward to it. When I first arrived at the farm, there were too many things to do for me to stick around the house all the time. I noticed every day that about eleven o'clock in the morning, Bessie would come out of the house, look around, and slowly walk to the front gate. She then turned left and strolled down the gravel driveway toward the road a few hundred feet away. It took a few days for me to notice that she was not just taking a stroll. After reaching the county road she went to the mailbox. The postman had arrived. That was the car that I saw pass the barn area and move to the south, down the road. Bessie was getting the mail. Again I didn't think too much about it until the next day when I watched Bessie perform her ritual. This time I watched more closely. She reached the road, opened the mail box after putting the red flag out of sight. She first looked into the open box, then she thrust her hand inside and pulled out some letters. After looking them over she put her hand back inside and pulled out something larger than a letter. Slowly she opened what she had in her hand and began looking at the outstretched pages. Why was she looking at it in the middle of the road, I wondered? What could be so important that she couldn't wait until she was back at her kitchen table to look at it. Suddenly, I realized what this absorbing thing was. It was a newspaper.

The postman brought the newspaper as well as letters to the farmer. The Argus Leader newspaper was the most common newspaper that people subscribed to, and it was the choice of Ed and Bessie.

After discovering this wonderful addition to the lonely existence on the farm, I would spend hours looking over the comics, feature pages, and news of the region. Although I knew I would not be going anywhere to see them, it was fabulous being able to find out all of the events of the area from the newspaper.

The arrival of the newspaper became the most looked to event on the farm.

..............................

In Sioux Falls my family always had a garden. On Eighth Avenue we had a complete lot to the south of the house. On Third Avenue, it was in the back yard. Because we had houses next to ours now, the plot on Third Avenue was smaller than that on Eighth Avenue.

Dad and Mom planted carrots, peas, beans, radishes, tomatoes, and potatoes mainly. I remember my Dad having a man with a horse and a hand-plow coming to turn up the dirt in this large plot on Eighth Avenue. It was big lot and ploughing took half a day. The man then dragged a large metal frame with spikes over the clumps to loosen and spread them out. When it was smooth, we took our hoes and made a small open row to plant the seeds of our vegetables in it. It was not the type of activity that we kids liked. It was a boring job and took too much time of our play time. Much of our time was spent waiting for Dad or Mom to decide on which thing to plant and where. Our minds would continually wander away from our task and Dad sometimes had to give us a 'box' on the ear to bring us back to the task at hand.

When I went to the farm near Rowena, I knew that I wouldn't be asked to help plant the garden as it had already been planted by Ed and Bessie. It was not too far from the house, behind a fence that kept the chickens out. Ed and Bessie worked well together on things like this and they loved planting the garden together. I could tell that they were proud of their garden and their achievement by the way they talked about it. They knew when different vegetables were going to sprout and be ready to eat. They talked quite often about the garden that first summer.

Ed was easy to talk to, and he loved to "shoot the bull" with people. Friends were always dropping by to talk to him. He was a good carpenter and he would help others solve their problems and in turn he would get information about the things that needed to be done on the farm.

One afternoon I noticed that he was talking to a neighbor out by the barn. I was interested in what they were talking about so I strolled out to where they were and listened. It was a general conversation about the weather, the cows he had and their health, and other farm things in general. Suddenly Ed looked at me and asked me if I would go to the garden and get a watermelon. It was kinda hot and he thought it would taste good as well as satisfy our thirst. Sure, I told him. Look around and pick a good one, one large enough for the three of us, and he resumed his conversation with the neighbor.

Closing the gate behind me, I went into the yard where the garden was. I began looking around for a large, ripe watermelon, one that would taste good for the three of us. I looked and I looked. I couldn't find any ripe watermelons, but I kept walking around the "patch" and looked. Ed said they were ripe, so there must be at least one around somewhere. Looking back toward the barn, I noticed Ed and the neighbor looking at me in the watermelon patch. I kept looking. I lifted up the leaves to make sure I missed none. I couldn't find a ripe one after I had looked over the entire watermelon patch at least three times.

Exasperated, I finally gave up. I could not find any ripe melons in the patch. Out of the corner of his eye I noticed that Ed and his friend were coming toward me. Frustrated and embarrassed, I explained that I didn't find a ripe melon for them. The melons were not ripe to eat yet I said. They are still too green. I felt I had failed them. As soon as I got the words out, they looked at each other and burst out laughing.

"They are supposed to be green," Ed said. "That means they are ripe."

I felt smaller than a worm. Green! I never noticed before. The outside is green, but the inside is red. What a fool I was. I had never been asked to pick a watermelon before at home. Dad or Mom always had done this chore.

Another lesson I would never forget.

*Dream when you're feeling blue...........*

# 19
# Longfellow

When the family moved from Eighth Avenue to Third Avenue, we had to go to Longfellow Elementary School.

Longfellow School was built on a slightly rolling mound of the prairie in 1916. The one-story school was beautifully designed with a Mediterranean flavor and constructed with running bond brick structure. The dark brown color contrasted with the immediate neighborhood of mainly white two-story wooden homes and this gave it a rich flavor of texture and distinctiveness. Its construction was to be the answer to the developing needs of the rapidly expanding prairie city in the McKennan Park-Boulevard-Galesburg- Addition area. Gales Addition (Galesburg) had been platted in l870, but it's real growth and the Boulevard Addition of his sister, Mrs. Helen McKennan, occurred from l900 to the 1920s. But alas, it became woefully small as the population grew in this area. The solution: expand by building more rooms and a gymnasium. Longfellow School had to have an addition of l8 rooms in l932 before it finally caught up with the student population increase.

..............................

Summer was here!

"What do I do now?"

I was on my own. It was many times harder on the parents to adjust to this free time than for the children who welcomed the opportunity to sleep late, play, swim, and explore throughout the community.

Actually, I had grown to like being at the school during the year. I welcomed the interplay amoung me, the teachers, and my buddies. I had finally found an area where my achievements of leadership and intelligence were recognized by many of the teachers, even though my social graces were not what they desired. Although I was a born leader and well liked by almost all of the kids, I had at times a very caustic and abrasive attitude. I could be a likable person, but when somebody challenged me my personality changed drastically. I could become belligerent and ruthless because of the competitive nature and attitude I had developed in order to survive in a large household. This nature of my personality had developed early but it was hidden by my pleasant nature. I was a good-looking kid, with blond hair and large features that I would later develop with weightlifting. I realized early in life that good looks and personality were a decided advantage.

The first days of adjustment after the ending of the school year were days of suspended animation. I felt that I was in limbo. I acted like a zombie when suddenly I was dropped out of the school routine. One day I was actively orientated and now my pace became slow and indistinct. My goals had been halted.

Due to the habit of nine months of conditioning, I found myself walking back to the school grounds. Maybe there had been a mistake. Actually I was hoping to run across one of my buddies. I was lonely.

The few blocks back to the school ground seemed never to end. The shades on many of the windows were drawn. The building was deserted. No lights were visible in the vacated halls. The playground was vacant. The swings and the monkey bars were empty. The swings had been the most sought-after objects at recess for the past nine months, but now they stood empty and forlorn. Out of habit, I raced to the swings and grabbed the first one. There was no joy in getting them so easy and after swinging for a few minutes, guilt crept over me. I felt cheated. It was a hollow victory. There was no one to argue with me. It was too easy. The competitiveness of being first was gone. It's not nearly as much fun unless you can argue about those things. Whether you win the argument or not is not important. The hunt is many times more fun than the kill.

The swing became boring so a new activity had to be sought. After slowly looking around, I ambled over to the brick building to satisfy a curiosity. After stretching to look into the windows which were about at the height of my head, I began searching for the new classroom I would be in next year. It proved futile because I had temporarily forgotten who my new teacher would be. Makes no difference, I thought, I'll just look in all of the windows instead. Mrs. McMurtchie's music window was easy to identify as it protruded from all of the rest of the classrooms. I eagerly peered into the gloomily dark interior. Although she was a hard teacher and a harsh taskmaster, Mrs. McMurtchie was a good teacher and well-remembered. Much to my surprise, I liked the music lessons I had taken. The music classes were the most popular with the kids and rightly so, as it was the type of class a person with my personality could feel free to open my mouth and vent my opinion and feeling in a vocal media. The songs that were sung were interesting and invigorating. This activity released a great deal of the pent-up energy that the students had been unable to release in the academic classes. The music teacher was a well-respected person, as every one knew she put out a lot of effort and took a lot of guff from the too-large class when they were trying to learn songs. It had to be extremely frustrating for her at times. When all of the long hours of practice was over, a beautiful well-understood song could be shared with all of the community. This was one class in the school that would reap dividends for many years. Much of the music appreciation gained in these classes hung with the students and affected them for their entire lives. Stillness was the only thing in the room now. No beautiful vocal sounds came forth now that summer was here.

Where to go now? The boiler room roof? Yes. The next place to visit had to be the top of the boiler room. Here was one of the most popular play areas of the school. It was a large, flat area suitable for developing the running skills of the students. It was a fabulous area that beckoned kids before school, during recess, and after school. It was a wonderful area to challenge your rivals. Here was where running games were invented at all times of the day—before school, during recess and occasionally after school. The cement top of the boiler room turned out to be ideal for games. Everyone congregated in the area in the morning as it was close to the swings and monkeybars. Leaders were chosen from the first ones interested, and they chose sides to develop a team...and the races began. Everyone could compete in these games because the winner wasn't always the fastest or strongest person. The winner many times was the person in the best position to outwit the fastest when he was distracted by the other runners. Everybody became a winner in these made-up foot races.

Just below the roof where the races were run was the heartbeat of the school heating plant, the boiler room. The inside of the boiler room was always a fascinating and interesting place. It was a huge room with a high roof that had pipes of all sorts clinging to it. There was always the deafening roar of the coal burners that had now been converted into oil burners. Peering into the burners was an awe-inspiring event that only a few bold ones dared to do. The heat was unbearable and the noise was terrifying. Needless to say, the area was off limits unless accompanied by the supervisor, Mr. Simpson. He was the authority in this area and his word was supreme. His was a familiar face around the school and everyone respected him. It didn't take long to realize that you had better be nice to him if you wanted to survive in the cold days of the winter. It was not always easy to coordinate your arrival to school to coincide with the opening of the front doors. On the winter mornings this could bring a great degree of discomfort if you arrived before the front doors were opened. On extremely cold days it was horrible standing outside in the cold. As more and more kids huddled next to the boiler door Mr. Simpson took pity on the student's cold condition and opened the normally closed boiler room door and let them stand on the metal steps that led to the bottom of the boiler room. As a special favor to me and my friend Ted who had both moved away from the adjacent area of Longfellow School, Mr. Simpson let both of us eat our lunch in the boiler room during the last year of school there.

I strolled to the unpaved playground to the east of the school. This was a large dirt area of many acres for snowball fights and general congregation.

Looking back toward the east side of the brown brick school, one can see the two entrances with the gym between them. The large, tall, gym windows were ten feet off the ground and the only way to look into the gym was by climbing a cement lip under the windows. It was a feat of dexterity and skill, but it could be done and after getting up to the window sill one had to hold on like mad so you wouldn't fall. This was a favorite place to go to see who was in the gym at night. Here was where the Friendly Indians met once a week, in the evening. The Friendly Indians was organized by the YMCA as a recreational activity. After the hour or so of play in the gym, the group went to someone's house for cookies and lemonade. Everyone had to have the group in the house at one time during the year, and I dreaded this time. My mother was so ill now that her bed had been placed in the front room so she could be helped easier. The director of Friendly Indians, however, never asked me to have the group to my house, much to my relief.

The planter below the windows was dirt that never had any grass or flowers in it. The entrance to the north was raised about six feet above the sloping playground. There were steps up to a cement courtyard that led to the metal door. Here was where we waited in a crowd listening for the sound of the janitor to unlock the door and pull off the metal chain that was wrapped around the push bar on the door. This was the area that teasing, some name calling, and shoving took place while waiting for the door to open. This was the place where young innocent Marcy exclaimed one day "Look at the doggies—they're doing the rumba." Not being a man of the world, even I knew at my young age that the dogs were not doing the rumba.

As the north side of the school was given its final check, I slowly walked back home to idle away the summer.

..............................

"What? What did you say, Mrs Slater?" I had suddenly been shaken out of my soul as somewhere in the distance I heard our English teacher, Mrs. Slater, bark out a command. The new semester had begun and I had been assigned the seat by the window. The seat was both a godsend and a bane to me as I enjoyed looking out. I, however, sometimes got carried away and would drift into a peaceful, soma state, akin to a trance.

I now felt the presence of her large frame between me and the outdoor window.

"Fred, if you can come back to the classroom for one second," she asked sternly. The others around me were aware of her now and all of their attention was focused on the upcoming event they knew would make for a scene if I didn't control myself. "Fred, have it ready by Friday. You can recite it at the lunch hour. I will be here." and she briskly turned and strode back to the front of the room. "Now pay attention to what is going on."

Recite? Recite what? She must have told me something and I didn't hear it. What though? Now I was not only embarrassed but also perplexed.

Suddenly, hardly taking my eyes off Mrs. Slater in the front of the room, I noticed the paper on my desk. It was one sheet of paper with a lot of typed words on it. Quickly I glanced at it. It was a poem, a long poem. I placed my hand under my chin unobtrusively, and slowly let my eyes focus on the sheet.

The title at the top of the page was "*If.*"

*If?* what kind of a title is that. I have to memorize this thing, by Friday noon? I started counting the lines. one.......ten..........twenty.....Oh, my God. It doesn't quit.

*If you can keep your head, when all about you.* Keep my head, why should I lose it? Oh, my God.

*Are losing theirs and blaming it on you.* Yeah, I'd like to catch anyone blaming something on me that I didn't do. He wouldn't do it again, I'll assure you.

The bell rang and we moved to the best class of the day, physical education. I could be king there. I was bigger than everyone in the class, I was more coordinated than anyone in the class, and I was the best in the class. The only thing I didn't like about the class was the teacher. She was always picking on me. She never left me alone.

"Fred, remember: Friday noon. Don't forget. I'll be here." Mrs Slater shouted at me as I avoided getting near her and passed out of the door away from her desk in the front of the room.

Hey, If you can keep your head when all about you, are losing theirs and blaming it on you. I remembered.

The hall was crowded. A quick glance at the paper: *If you can trust yourself when all men doubt you, But make allowance for their doubting too?* Make allowance for their doubting too?

*If you can wait and not be tired by waiting, Or, being lied about, don't deal in lies.* I don't lie! There is no need to lie. Be truthful and the truth will out. Where did I hear that? Wait, don't go anywhere you will have to wait. That's simple enough.

The hall congestion improved and I reached the gym. It was to be a day of throwing the volleyball and hitting the other team members. I like that. I can throw better than anyone. I can dodge better than anyone. I like this game. I usually win.

*If you can keep your head when all around you, are losing theirs and blaming it on you. If you can trust yourself when all men doubt you, But make allowance for their doubting too.*

Those lines keep going through my head. Bam, the ball resounded off the wall behind me, but it didn't hit me.

"You can't hit me," I shouted to the other end of the gym, but before I had finished the sentence, the ball hit me.

"You're out, Fred. Sit down." The teacher commanded.

"What do you mean he hit me. He missed me. Didn't he miss me, Jim?" as I pleaded to the boy sitting on the sidelines. No answer.

"Sit down, Fred!"

Dejected, I went to the side of the gym and sat down on the hard wood floor. I was furious. The others in the class had taken new positions against the wall now and the ball was again flying from one end of the large gym to the other.

The paper Mrs. Slater had given to me was in my pocket and I took it out. I began reading again.

*If you can wait and not be tired by waiting, Or, being lied about, don't deal in lies.*

*Or be hated, don't give way to hating, And yet don't look too good, nor talk too wise.* Yeah, well he doesn't know anything about losing. I could tell him something about losing. Hating. Huh. I don't hate anyone, but nobody had better try me.

*If you can dream— and not make dreams your master; If you can think— and not make thoughts your aim;* That's dumb. If you can dream and not make dreams your master.

*If you can meet with triumph and disaster and treat those two imposters just the same.* Triumph and disaster? Imposters. Treat them just the same? Triumph and disaster—I just want triumph. You stay away from disaster. What does that mean, treat them both the same? Triumph means winning, that's what I'm supposed to do. I'm going to win. I need to win. I will win. Treat them both the same. Haw.

Walking home, alone, was the best time of the day. The leaves were falling and made a crunch when you stepped on them. There was a slight smoke smell of burned leaves in the air. It was a restful, peaceful time of day—walking between school and home.

I took the paper out of my pocket and began reading where I had left off: *If you can make one heap of all your winnings and risk it on one turn of pitch-and-toss.* Gamble? Not me. You can lose too easily. *And lose, and start again at your beginnings And never breathe a word about your loss.* You bet I wouldn't tell anyone. But I'm not dumb enough to bet everything on anything. Only a loser does that. You know, I said to myself, this poem isn't too bad. A little dumb, but not too bad.

*If you can force your heart and nerve and sinew to serve your turn long after they are gone, and so hold on when there is nothing in you except the Will which says to them: "Hold on."*

At this point I glanced at the bottom of the page and read the last few lines.

*If you can fill the unforgiving minute with sixty seconds' worth of distance run—Yours is the Earth and everything that's in it,*

*AND—WHICH IS MORE—YOU'LL BE A MAN, MY SON.*

Rudyard Kipling

So that's it? That's all?

I got home and entered my house.

"Hi, mom. How are you today?"

A faint smile appeared on the gaunt face of the person lying on the bed in the front room. It was a weak smile, but it was warm.

Soon the warmth would fade from that smile forever.

...............................

As I approached the teenage years and after my mother's death, I stopped attending church. The church had ceased to be a part of my life. Or so I thought. Questions of 'life' and 'the path to travel' continually plagued me and made my life sometimes extremely confusing. My mother had been taken by God, so I was told. 'It was for the best,' as God had a greater need for her than I did. Why? I couldn't understand this. There were eight children in the family that now had no mother to love or guide them. Children who needed their mother. Why was God's need more important than ours? It didn't make sense. The answers weren't satisfying to me. I had to now find my way alone, so I thought.

As I got older, my body as well as my mind had continued to change. My body was maturing, and I was getting urges that I had never felt before. My confusion continually haunted me. In my loneliness and isolation now, I started attending Sunday services at a different church from the one that my parents had taken me to. Motives were twofold for me at this time, however. The continual quest for answers about life and success were paramount in my mind as I still did not feel confident about either. The second motive concerned the attraction of the opposite sex. The girls that attracted and fascinated me attended church. No matter that I was too shy to approach them, they could be seen during the services and that was enough to satisfy my teenager biological awakenings.

All females held a fascination for boys at this age, but for me the church-going ones held a special fascination. They all smelled fresh and wore beautiful, clean clothes. This thought permeated my direction—clean-clothed people succeeded. Unclean people had less of a chance of gaining faith, direction, and success. I began dressing up more often and I felt successful and confident. This became a focus of living for me.

But the lingering doubts of acceptance and future success still annoyed me. Although I felt I could be accepted and succeed, the question of having the faith that every one of these ritualists had attained I still didn't have.

More and more my analysis of the rituals and arguments that produced many of these faithful, produced a faith of a different type in me. Confidence in myself and my direction grew stronger the more I rejected the formalized pursuit of faith. Their faith had given me more faith in myself and my outlook on life. I grew to realize that it was the outlook of the individual that really mattered. If you felt good about yourself, that would produce faith and success. The external manifestations of clothing and hair style were not the only criteria for well-being.

Apparently the formalized approach by these people that had sometimes badgered me about their religion had succeeded, but not as they had envisioned or desired.

I had rejected their formal rituals. I could formulate arguments for my behavior and then justify them myself. That was not what the formalists wanted, but it satisfied and guided me. I had finally arrived at my personal state of faith.

This was to be my direction for life. And it worked.

Faith in myself became the first step to success. All other things would follow.

*Going to take a slow boat to China All by myself alone.........*

# 20
# Sport Bowl-The Whizzer

My mother passed away in August, 1944. I was 11 years old.

The Second World War was nearing its fourth year and the Army Air Base in Sioux Falls was in full operation. Thousands of soldiers were being trained at the Air Base in radio techniques. All work and no play......in their off hours they sought entertainment. The downtown Sport Bowl on Phillips Avenue offered bowling as well as arcade entertainment. The arcade part of the entertainment included pin ball machines, scooter ball, skill games, and the usual 'coney island' entertainment as well as a novelty shop that sold souvenirs for the folks back home. A small cafe was available to get food and socialize over cups of coffee. The Sport Bowl was where all of the action was and it was a good place to meet girls. It was not considered a proper place for the good young girls of the community to be seen in, however.. It attracted what many thought to be the riff-raff, or the young thrill seekers out for a lark. Much of the soldiers' spare time was spent in the Sport Bowl, as it was a very popular place.

The Sport Bowl had 16 alleys on its two floors and pinsetters were always in demand. It was physical work to set pins. There were no automatic pin setting devices in 1944 and the ten pins had to be set up by hand. Mainly young boys and a few older men did this type of work, and occasionally women did work there.

The pin setters got five cents a line (game) for open bowling and league play. The bowlers paid twenty-five cents per game to play except for league play, which was a little higher. A league team had five players on it and they competed against another team of five players. The first league teams started playing at seven o'clock in the evening and they bowled three games each for a total of thirty games. About nine o'clock the first league was done and the second began its contest. This lasted until a little after eleven o'clock when another thirty games were completed. Thus three dollars could be made setting one lane. Double that if you were able to set two lanes.

My friend, Ted, had started working at the Sport Bowl while in the seventh grade while attending Longfellow School. He talked me into trying it out also. After a few months as a pinsetter, I started working regularly on Monday, Wednesday, and Friday leagues for a total of setting 180 games. At 5 cents a game this earned me a total of nine dollars. I then began working Saturday and Sunday to earn another ten to twelve dollars. A paycheck of twenty dollars for the week was a good paycheck for a twelve-year old. With this money I bought my clothes, food at work, and anything I needed to go to school. I was essentially on my own after my mother's death in 1944 and this money was necessary to support myself.

Work finished around eleven o'clock. Any child working after the curfew had to be given transportation home. The management gave a bus token for a ride home. Many nights I walked home rather than spend the token. I saved a dime.

On Saturday nights the open bowling usually lasted until one or two o'clock in the morning—too late to catch the bus home. After all of the alleys were finished with their activity, a cab was called and all the pinsetters that hadn't gone by then were piled into the cab for delivery home. The first setters to finish work had to wait until all of the bowling was finished before the cab was called. They would sometimes finish one or two hours before the cab would be called. Everybody were tired. It was hard work setting pens and all they wanted was rest or at least a place to close their eyes. The boys many times fell asleep sitting in some corner on the floor. This half-asleep, half-awake feeling was especially uncomfortable. When the cab finally arrived, all had to pile into the one and only cab they had ordered. Two cabs were never ordered. Although it was probably illegal, ten to twelve kids would be in the cab. The luckiest kids were the ones who got to the cab first and sat in the front seat. Only two were allowed to sit in the front seat by the driver. Once everyone was inside the cab, the ordeal of determining the shortest route for the driver to take was begun. If it was a really late night everyone wanted to get home first. After eight to ten minutes of kids shouting addresses out to the driver, the cab finally took off for the trip home. Many times the last kid got home around three o'clock.

The pinsetting area was very noisy, dusty, and dangerous. Shortly after starting work at the Sport Bowl, I was hit square in the nose by a pin that had bounced up from the alley. I saw a few stars for a while and it felt like my nose was broken. It was. I wasn't sent to a doctor for what seemed like a small inconvenience injury but after a few days I discovered that the pin had chipped my two front teeth. This was not taken care of and the decay later caused a abscess and the two front teeth had to be pulled.

Although today we may consider this type of work for teenagers unsuitable, we welcomed it at the time, as it was one of the few chances for a kid to make some money. Not many opportunities were available to the kids of the '40s.

In spite of the long hours working next to each other, a certain camaraderie developed between the pinsetters. There was time to play with the new-found buddies at the Sport Bowl. Saturday mornings was a slow time and that was when the group would mosey on down to the falls and seek fun. We left by way of the back door of the bowling alley, across the railroad

*The Sioux falls at low water. (Charles Fredricks photo)*

tracks, down between the International Harvester warehouse on Sixth Street and then cut back toward the falls. There was a train trestle to the south of the falls and it was used as a resting bench. A good place to view the area could be had from here also. It was on one of these pauses on the trestle that I decided to quit smoking cigarettes. Most of the other kids smoked and it seemed the right thing to do. I had tried smoking cigarettes off and on for a couple of months after starting work at the Sport Bowl. Because the war was on, the cigarettes were not available all of the time due to the war shortages. The armed services had priority on the 'cancer sticks' and the civilian public was rationed. Whenever they did arrive for sale at the Sport Bowl, Tommy the clerk would treat them like packages of gold and he doled them out with great care. They were never sold openly and this added to the mystique for me. They cost fifteen cents a pack in those days, a lot of money then. Almost everyone I knew smoked them.

"Hey, Fred, you got a cigarette? Let me have one. I'll pay you back when I get some," someone shouted.

"Yeah, sure. Remember you owe me," I replied. "Fat chance I'll get repaid," I said to myself.

After a few months of smoking cigarettes, I decided that they were costing me too much money. Every time I had a pack of butts, like a magnet all of my buddies found me and bummed a couple off me. I ended up with an empty pack and I was fifteen cents poorer. Enough of this, I thought. The way to stop this practice was to not practice it. I felt better after making the decision to quit smoking.

Sitting on the railroad trestle was a peaceful experience. The falls were beautiful. And a challenge. When the smoke break was over, we would pursue our fun by jumping over chasms of rock, puddles of pounded water, and generally goofing off. If it was hot, we would peel off our clothes and wade into shallow pools of water...or deeper water if we were really brave. A few of the braver ones jumped off some of the smaller falls. We never jumped or swam around the largest and most powerful fall. The biggest and classic fall that everyone sees was just too dangerous and menacing even for us. Later in life when I viewed the falls at an extremely low phase of drought, I was appalled at the number of boulders at the base of most of the falls that we had jumped off into the water below. God must have been looking over us or we were extremely lucky. Probably both things were true.

Lunches were never taken along on these excursions and there were no cafes around, but a few blocks away was the Crescent Creamery where ice cream could be bought. With a flip of the coin, it would be decided as to who would walk to the former brewery on Main and buy a pint of ice cream for each of us. Eating ice cream after an exhausting morning of play was truly heaven. Hot and tired from our excursion to the falls, the delectable, delicious ambrosia of the gods was our reward.

..............................

The war was over, but the supply of automobiles and other mechanized vehicles had not caught up with the demand of the consuming public. I wanted some means of transportation to get around as I was tired of having to walk everywhere. My job at the Sport Bowl gave me more money than I had ever had. Some was used for spending money—for food, my own clothes that I bought now, and school paper—and I was able to save some of it. Thanks to Mr. Hilker, the manager of the Sport Bowl, who had set up an account of one dollar in a local savings bank for a Christmas present, I had been introduced to systematically saving money. I was the first person in my immediate family who had ever started an account in a bank, thanks to the generosity of Mr. Hilker. This small gesture of one dollar by Mr. Hilker was to greatly influence my saving and spending practices for the rest of my life.

*The Whizzer motor bike opened many avenues of adventure to me. (FF Collection) (Photo taken at the 15th and Elmwood Avenue basement house.)*

I was very conservative with money. The challenge of saving money, taking it to the bank and depositing it became a ritual that I embraced fully. Before long I had saved $150. One hundred and fifty dollars. It seemed like a million dollars to a thirteen-year old.

The chore of walking everywhere was getting to be drudgery, and it took a lot of my time. I hated waiting for busses that never came, or missed busses that took a lot of time out of my day. Now that I had money I could solve my transportation problems. But a car would cost too much. Gas, tires, license....too much money. After much thought about the type of transportation needed, I decided that I could afford something cheaper—a Whizzer Motor Bike. I had seen a few of these bicycles and the ease of handling and convenience impressed me. Storm's Bicycles, next to Metz Baking Company on the East Side, sold these bikes. After numerous visits to check them out, I finally decided to buy one.

The Whizzer Motor Bike I bought was nothing more than a regular Schwinn bicycle with a small one-cylinder engine mounted between the bars where the bar frame formed a closed 'V' between the seat and the handle bars. The one-gallon gas tank was mounted forward of the seat with the motor mounted below it between your legs. A belt ran to the rear wheel from a pulley on the motor and this provided the power to make the bike go. To start the motor, the bicycle had to be pedaled like a regular bike, and this turned the motor over. There was no electric starter on the bike. Spark had to be given to the motor before it would start, and the gas was regulated from a lever on the handlebars. When the engine didn't start, the bike could be ridden like a regular bike, but it was harder to pump it this way.

The Whizzer gave me an exhilarating sense of freedom that I had never dreamed possible. Zooming down the road at 30 to 40 miles per hour created a glorious sense of adventure that I pushed to the fullest. The miles of highway to Renner, Canton, Shindler, Rowena, and other exotic places were now in reach for this adventurer to explore. Up and down hills, across valleys, around every block in the city I went on the Whizzer. It was a glorious and wondrous world to explore. I left no horizon untouched while I had the Whizzer. I had to see it all. I *needed* to see it all. The world *needed* exploring and I was the Christopher Columbus of Sioux Falls.

..............................

But had I done everything?

In 1947, having conquered the Valley of the Sioux with the Whizzer, the challenge of going to the Black Hills on my bike, over 300 miles away, inflamed my mind. The idea was generated by Bill Zayer, a buddy at Washington High School, when he told me that he was going with his parents to the Black Hills that summer. Wouldn't it be great if they could rendezvous at Mt. Rushmore?

Sounds good to me, I thought, giving no thought to the actual distance to the Black Hills, or to whether I could get there on my Whizzer.

The challenge was too great to be ignored. Early on a summer morning with my sleeping bag and a few clothes tied to the bike carrier, and a little money in my pocket, I left home on the trip to the Black Hills.

The trip began uneventfully. The day was clear, no rain or clouds in sight, and it was beautiful with an expected warming up to occur by afternoon.

What a day to be traveling. With the wind in my hair, no problems in the world, and a few bucks in my pocket, I felt I was on top of the world. The Whizzer hummed smoothly as I set my sights for the West. Ten miles, twenty miles, forty miles....the miles melted away. However as I neared Mitchell, the engine started running a little rough. It wasn't real bad but it concerned me. There were few towns as large as Mitchell further west so I decided to check it out in Mitchell before going on. No luck. A person who knew a little about Whizzers couldn't help me. I convinced myself that there was no big problem. It would smooth itself out, I told myself. I wasn't going to let anything as minor as motor trouble stop me and my mission. I decided to push on.

As I left Mitchell I noticed that the bike wasn't going as fast as it had been going. Odd. However, the overwhelming urge to travel and the wide-open road kept me going. The stop in Mitchell had taken off some of the edge of the adventure and although I didn't want to dwell on it too much, I began to have a slight sinking feeling in my stomach. I wasn't totally oblivious to the possibility of failure. I knew that Rapid City was a far way off and almost anything could happen before I made it. As I continued down the two lane highway my worst fear began to become more evident. The engine began running rougher. The speed decreased. The trouble grew worse, and I now became very concerned. White Lake was only a few miles away. No cars had passed me in a half-hour.I began praying I could make it before the engine gave out. Five miles to go. Three miles to go. Keep going I prayed. The town came into sight. One mile to go. I now knew this was the end of the trip. White Lake would be the last stop.

By the time I reached the town, the Whizzer was barely running. A flat crankshaft was the problem, a service station attendant informed me as he listened to the engine. The attendant could do nothing for me. And there is nobody else around here that can fix it. The adventure that had started out only hours before was finished.

What to do? I looked around. Checking at the train depot, I found out that the train ran through the town, but not until tomorrow. 'You could ship the bike back to Sioux Falls,' the station-keeper said. That's it, I'll send it back on the train. That would take care of the Whizzer but I couldn't wait around for a day to get back to Sioux Falls. Suddenly the solution came to me. Although I had never hitch-hiked before, I would try hitch-hiking back. Slowly I walked toward the road and began putting my thumb out as cars passed by. Another adventure.

It was a great idea. The failure of the adventure didn't bother me in the least.

What a day.

*Red sails in the sunset...........*

***1947 Longfellow Elementary School Mid-Year Graduation***

*Top Row: Billy Onenga, Walt Lease, Ron Ryan, James Tyler, Hary Mitchell, Chuck Simpson, Gerald Warren, Johnny McLaughlin, Don Eide, Paul Arnopoulos; Middle Row: Dick Neish, Kenny Malloy, Ted Beuchens, Bill Lowe, Dick Fredricks, Don Modica, Ron Richardson, Leonard Blackburn, Miss Girton; Bottom Row: Bill Zaayer, Marcella Tripp, Marlene Micheals, Ruth Howalt, LaVon Polzien, Joanne Dedrick, Shirley Paul, Jim McLaughlin.*

# 21
# Washington High School

The pangs of youth and adjustment to social conformity develop in strange and unexpected ways in a child. They have the continual feeling that everyone in the world is always looking at them and judging them. Youth. Everyone thought they were the only ones that were having these problems and the world seemed like it would never quit making excessive demands on them. Leave me alone! When would it all stop? Life was not supposed to be this cruel. When could we enjoy ourselves?

At Longfellow Grade School the kids did the usual rough house things that kids do—wrestle, chase each other, and have snowball fights in winter. Born a natural leader, I developed a following of kids and they always wanted me as their leader in the athletic events they engaged in on the playground. The teams I led usually won the contests and everyone wanted to be chosen to be on 'my' team. It was easy for me to compete. I was a winner to them.

I matured rapidly. I was becoming larger and stronger. I was no longer the average Galesburg boy at Longfellow although I didn't know this at the time. I kept outgrowing my clothes. I kept putting on weight: 100 pounds, 110 pounds, 120 pounds. I kept getting bigger. And stronger. I had developed a 'attitude' look that told others that I wasn't to be messed with. And when I was challenged I would only have to look at the person to avoid physical confrontation. Only once, with regret, did I overpower and hurt a boy while playing at school. After that one incident, I never got into arguments or fights with other boys, except in play. I had noticed that the other boys never picked fights with me. They always shied away when I gave them "that look". Years later that I realized what my large size saved me from. As I reached 150 pounds of weight in the eighth grade my confidence had increased immensely.

While in seventh grade, my mother had died. This happened in August, 1944. and it almost tore the family apart. My father was always working, my mother was gone. Life was vacant. My sister, Dorothy, although only nineteen, began taking care of me and my brothers and sisters after there was talk of me being put into the Children's Home on Tenth Street.

School at Longfellow started in September. My buddy, Ted, was setting pins at the Sport Bowl bowling alley and he talked me into working there also. In October I started setting pins at the downtown Sport Bowl. It was a great challenge, a challenge that occupied my mind and body to the fullest. I loved it. I could satisfy both my need for success and my need to make some money. This greatly increased my stature... and strength. I was a rapid learner and I took to the challenge of working easily. It became too easy and I began looking around for a harder task. With newly-developed determination, strength, and coordination I took on the challenge of setting two alleys at a time—a feat few my age could accomplish. The job setting pins was what I had needed to get myself out of my self-pitying situation. This challenge became a move in a new direction for me. Along with my development of self-reliance, my sense of identity increased.

After my mother died, I felt totally alone. I had loved my mother and she had been a great companion to me. My personality changed. A new sense of worth developed in me. Life had been cruel, but I must go on. I wanted to do what I felt my mother would have wanted me to do. I began to feel and know that I was the only hope for maintaining myself and succeeding in high school and life. I began to realize that I had to chart my course myself. There was no one else to do this for me. I was in command. I was now the captain of my soul.

The struggle throughout life without a formalized education somehow didn't seem smart. I knew and sensed that I had to maintain a course different from the rest of the family. I knew my mother would have wanted me to continue school.

...............................

It was a cold January night when the mid-year graduates from Longfellow Elementary School marched into the auditorium at Washington High School. They were the members of the graduating class of 1947. Mr. Beck spoke sternly and eloquently. The usual speeches about loyalty to your new school, setting a example for the others that follow, and doing your best were given.

"Look at them," I said to myself as I leaned against the wall on second floor. "Look at their clothes. Better than I have, or will probably ever have. I had to borrow my brother's jacket for graduation. I didn't even own a white shirt. It was my father's. I kept telling myself at the graduation that if I keep seated maybe nobody would notice." I felt like the geek in my high-topped, 'farmer shoes'. They didn't go with the jacket. And the pants, they were my older brother's also. And now. Plaid 'lumber jack' shirts, though warm, didn't show the sophistication that the crowd in the cafeteria exhibited and my blue jeans looked too washed out and wrinkled next to the fine gabardine the crowd from Pender Lane wore. My clothes are an embarrassment that could not be denied or overcome by my exuberance or quick smile. Things would have to change if I was to fit in this new intellectual environment.

After I entered Washington High School in January of 1947, my strength and size increased beyond the normal and... I kept getting bigger and stronger. My clothes were getting harder and harder to fit when I shopped for clothes. Shirts were especially hard to fit on me as I now had very broad shoulders. My rapid body growth, coupled with lack of money to replace clothes that I was outgrowing, developed a deep seated embarrassment to me that upset and angered me.

..............................

Central School opened in 1879 on the edge of the recently platted Gales Addition in the densely populated business area in the center of the upcoming prairie metropolis which had reached the population of over 2000 in the Valley of the Sioux. Thousands of immigrants and land seekers had been attracted to the state by lures of the good life and land. Many were disappointed, but many stayed and settled on the land that speculators sold them. By 1900 the population of the city was over 10,000. This rapid influx of people left the facilities for government and especially the education of their children woefully inadequate. Already the facilities of two previously constructed wooden schools were being considered for replacement again. The new-found wealth of the city as a distribution center to the ranches and farmers became an immense source of pride to the founding fathers and citizens and with thoughts of unlimited progress for the future, they began considering erecting a monument to education that would impress all of the Heartland. Their plans were to be practical but grandiose. A wooden structure was considered, but rejected. This time quartzite from the surrounding quarries was the choice of building material and a $130,000, four-story, Neoclassical style of architecture was to be used. This would give the emerging city a style that was practical, classy, and permanent. A beautiful touch of class was added when some rare black granite from Lien Park was incorporated into the north entrance. This showed some real taste for the farming community, and it showed to the world that bold new ideas were welcome in this progressive community. After three additions to the building over the years, the final form was accomplished in the early 1930s. The buildings were magnificent. A showplace of the Heartland.

The area within walking distance around the school had responded favorably to its presence. Responding to the need of a repository of books and written knowledge, on Tenth and Dakota a beautifully structured Carnegie Library whose style is reminiscent of a Greek temple was constructed in 1903, also of native quartzite stone. No plastic and stainless steel for this beacon of knowledge. Row after row of challenging titles of books would keep an inquisitive student busy browsing almost forever it seemed.

*The Carnegie Library on Tenth Street contributed greatly to fulfilling the dreams of youth. (Courtesy Center for Western Studies)*

The world opened before anyone who accepted the invitation to inquire and feed the mind until it was full. You were never hurried to get out when you were mesmerized by these written sensations. Wonders would never cease to amaze the inquisitive mind. Here also was the place that many students found for the first time the Argus Leader and the Minneapolis Tribune newspapers waiting to be explored for news of distant peoples' worlds. Without these papers available to the curious, receptive but economically-strapped children, the world would have remained only a few blocks wide, as primitive man perceived it. With the newspapers and books, one could transcend time rapidly in a matter of minutes. But wait, there was more to this building. Intangible feelings were released. The library had a soothing quietness that was lacking in many homes, especially mine. Entirely different manners than I was used to were expected here. It took a number of visits before I realized that this quiet atmosphere was the expected mode of behavior. I found out that people could actually concentrate and think for hours on end if they chose to.

I felt rudderless, but I managed to take care of myself. I felt like I didn't fit in anywhere anymore, now that my mother was dead.

A little over a year after my mother died, the family moved to Fifteenth and Elmwood to live. The oldest sister took over the duties of my mother. Because of my strong attachment to my teachers and friends, I elected to finish my grade school education at Longfellow School, and this meant that for

*Washington High School offered the key to success in life to me and my classmates in the late 1940s. (Charles Fredricks)*

the last semester and a half I had to walk from the western part of the city to Longfellow.

After things had settled down after entering Washington High School, there were many new acquaintances made and my life began to look better for me.

In the '40s, the humongous open halls on the second and third floors of Washington High School provided a wonderful social experience for me. Before classes began in the morning and afternoon, almost everybody could congregate in the halls to socialize and get acquainted. At lunch many chose to meet in the school cafeteria, but most brought their lunch and ate in the classrooms provided next to these large halls. In the '50s these were converted into classrooms and the students lost forever a great tradition of community and comradeship that the halls encouraged.

When this people-watching activity in the large hall got boring, a walk throughout the rest of the huge four-story building was undertaken. First one hall was slowly walked, then after a trek up the marble steps between floors was taken, another new floor awaited exploration.

On your 'tour' you saw everyone. A meeting of the eyes or a quick nod of the head was all that was usually needed as you passed. Most names of these quick acquaintances were fuzzy or unknown and they would never be known, but their faces would be remembered forever.

What really drove the boys crazy was the sighting of a 'new' heartthrob during these brief encounters of the "tour". Comments were made, but you did not dare approach the new girl if your buddies were with you. You'd be teased to death if you showed any extra attention to a particular girl. That is, if you were a freshman or sophomore. By the time you were a wise old experienced junior or senior the name of the game was becoming quite a lot clearer and you started actively pursuing these 'chance' encounters. Still it was hard to get acquainted sometimes and pursue your new interest.

The huge, wide halls were not without their perils. The terribly self-conscious freshman girls hurried across these long open spaces trying to avoid the gazes of a desired undeclared heartthrob or potential boyfriend. By the time they became a senior they would learn to walk slower unobtrusively, but still self-conscious across these open spaces.

The downtown Central High School evolution into a complete square-block educational facility, called Washington High School, did not come about overnight and without direction. It was a product of time. This large downtown location was deemed the best to serve the needs of a centrally concentrated business-oriented community such as occurred in most communities. It was easily accessible by walking or by the numerous types of public transportation that evolved to serve the community over the years. Virtually all forms of city transportation passed within two or three blocks of this huge evolving facility. The main shopping area centered on Phillips and Main Avenue supplied many of the jobs of the community. The commute to work by either parent was also a convenient way for the children, the family, and their friends to hitch a ride to school safely and quickly. Parking for the school was minimal, but it wasn't necessary except for a facility as cars weren't readily available to very many students. A student with a car was a rare thing to see.

The monument to education on Main, Dakota, Eleventh, and Twelfth streets became a magnet to progress. Numerous downtown businesses benefited, like Dickenson Bakery and Confectionery, a modern Deli, which catered to the students' eating necessity and habits. Not content with the sack lunch that was brought from home, at noon a stroll out of the north door of WHS, across Eleventh Street, past the Greyhound gas station on the northwest corner and a few yards up Main Avenue brought you to a cornucopia of food. Most concoctions at the deli were never seen in the homes of most students and they excited the palate and curiosity of all. It was a culinary adventure of the highest type. After paying for the container of chile, stew, or potato salad, the slower return to school was engrossed in getting every bit of taste out of the paper container. This snack would have to satisfy the stomach until the end of school when either Kirks, Kresges 5 & 10 Lunch counter, or the Palace of Sweets/Lemmonds could be gotten to and pacify the hunger pains before going home in the afternoon. The endless, insatiable thought and quest for food to a teenager was a powerful force for him and the business community did a wonderful job in satisfying these hungers.

Directly to the east of the school on Main stood another provider of food—a dairy store. A counter provided a hurried snack of a roll and coffee to Tyler and me only seconds before the homeroom warning bell sounded. The reason why we timed their snack so close to the last bell was never clear, although the food seemed to taste better if eaten this way.

..............................

The week of attending class at school was over. Saturdays were welcomed for a much-needed break in the routine.

All of this free time presented another problem that was hard to cope with as a teenager. What now did we do with the free time? Money was scarce and although movies cost only ten to fifteen cents, with the cost of popcorn or candy, the movie cost would mount up. Besides, going to a movie was not always satisfying. It was too impersonal sitting in a dark room for two to three hours. It was impossible to see other kids or meet new ones, especially girls, in this darkened atmosphere.

As a freshman, I and many other kids at WHS quickly discovered that the YMCA was open to school kids in Sioux Falls on Saturday night. With great apprehension the first time, I took advantage of the opportunity to go to the YMCA soon after entering WHS in January, 1947. As I entered the basement door beneath the main doors of the second floor, one of the teachers, Mr. Muller, took my ten cents entrance fee, and waived me into the hall. I stood there. What to do now? On my right were open double doors. The room was dark, but music was coming from somewhere in the room. "Why don't you go dance? Lots of girls here tonight. That's the dance room." Mr. Muller offered. "Over there." And he pointed to two sets of double doors to my left, "Later on movies will be shown. There's bowling upstairs, and the swimming pool is open. The pool room is probably full by now, but you can play pool if you can get in." After glancing into the darkened dance room, I started walking up the steps to the second floor with the thought in mind that I would go swimming. I had been swimming in the Sioux River and I liked swimming, but I had not been in a pool that was in a building. "I wonder what it is be like to take a swim in the wintertime?"

This first night at the Teen Canteen at the YWCA was to become a Saturday night ritual for me during the next four years. Many great friendships were begun while strolling around the huge complex. The movies were a riot. All of them were old and rejects from the main movie theaters. The films kept breaking and this gave us opportunity to whoop it up when the lights were turned on while repairs were made. Many times the films were never completed due to breakages. Dances were very low-key. Most of the boys sat in chairs that were placed around the walls. It took a lot of courage to ask a girl to dance and I developed the courage only a few times. Sometimes it would take all evening to get this courage before the chosen one was approached for a dance. None of these liaisons resulted in a date however. That took too much courage.

The Teen Canteen was a very welcome and decent thing the community of Sioux Falls offered to the youth of the city.

................................

The lack of parking at Washington High School didn't pose a big problem until the prosperity of the late '40s occurred. In the '50s and '60s this change in the Sioux Valley society was to be one of the biggest factors that influenced the diversification of the educational sites throughout the entire area.

Prosperity paved the way for the ultimate American Dream of a chicken in every pot and two or more cars on the street. This socioeconomic factor probably more than any other factor increased the pressure to discontinue using the central site as an educational facility. The first and main considerations in the studies for alternative uses after its being vacated in 1992 was related to parking space for automobiles.

Our prosperous society was 'hooked' on the convenience and personal use of the automobile and this God-given right was not to be given up easily. They had become instrumental in dictating the direction of the development of our community. Malls succeeded because they offered the main ingredient for success: convenience of a place to park our numerous cars. And the development of new houses followed the malls, or was it the malls that followed the development of houses? This vicious cycle fueled itself with the consequent deterioration of the inner cities almost across the entire Heartland.

No matter what the original instigator was, the distance to the central high school increased with each new house being constructed and as new elementary schools were being built, the old centrally-located high school looked less and less favorable. Like an old flame, she appealed less and less as she got older, until the old quartzite buildings were abandoned as an educational facility in 1992.

The break with the past is now complete.

In the Fall of 1992, a new modern Washington High School opened on a large expanse of a former farm east of Sioux Falls at Sixth and Sycamore. This move culminated after many years of concern by the school board about providing adequate space, modern facilities, and a more accessible school for the changing demographic character of the Sioux area which had reached a population of over 100,000. The old Highway 38 that took one from Sioux Falls to Valley Springs and beyond had been ripped out for the progress of this area and new streets have been built to accommodate the housing explosion that had been going on in the area for many years. The past still persists not too far away. The aging Lakeside Dairy buildings still remain across the highway to the east to remind the City fathers that their roots were built on farming of the prairie. The other traces of farms, however, were lost in the dust of the new roads and houses.

Too far along to ignore now, the people of the city had been moving onto the once-fertile farmlands that surrounded the core city of Sioux Falls. Decisions had to be made by the School Board. In 1965 Lincoln High School was constructed and this was the first overt attempt to keep up with the recent rapid changes of population in the Sioux Valley. The elementary schools were overcrowded. Washington High School was bursting at its seams with students. It had been a long time coming and it was not completed too soon for the thousands of future students that were to pass through its doors. This new thrust into the future would develop a new tradition for the students of the Sioux Valley.

## Eighth Grade Graduation, Sioux Falls Public Schools
## Washington High School Auditorium
## January 21, 1947 — 8:00 p.m.

### EMERSON SCHOOL

Helen Mae Anderson
Oliver R. Drymon
Betty J. Fideler
Ronald Greenslate
Arlene Joyce Groepel
Val Rae Hill
Marilyn J. Holly
Richard Alan Kinsley
Donna Jean Kirkeby
Paul Kolb
Raymond J. McCoun
Robert R. Meyers
Joyce Joan Moon
Donna N. Murray
John Norberg
Rose Anna Patterson
Richard C. Reid
Ralph J. Scott
Robert Skinlo
Donald L. Smith
Warren L. Stone
Robert R. Walton
Robert Todd Wagner

### HAWTHORNE SCHOOL

DeEtta Rae Anderberg
Corlus J. Austin
Betty Bonrud
Shirley L. Callies
Robin Jacquelyn Coon
Florence J. Granum
Rose Marie Hansen
Lyle Hanson
Donna Mae Hoellwarth
George Hofeditz
Roger L. Hoier
Helen Johnson
Betty Lee Jurgensen
Beverly E. Larsen
James E. Montis
Evelyn Perkins
Bonnie Phelps
John Edward Rezac
Rolland Floyd Stuckey
Maurice L. Tate
Vernon Thompson
Eugene Tuttle

### LINCOLN SCHOOL

Russell James Anderson
Marlene Burl Baker
Dale Clair Bergman
Kenneth Boom
Jeanette Pauline Doese
Donald Lee Ginther
LaValle Donald Gravning
Cliffrod Allen Jamison
Edward Dick Jensen
Ila June Larson
Richard Allen Merrill
Patricia Louise Nielsen
Larry Allen Pease
Clinton Gerald Philips
Allan Clifford Puckett
Edith Blanche Puckett
George William Sachen
Jerry Michael Schryver
James Lee Unzicker
Thomas M. Vick
Wayne Roger Wheelhouse

### LOWELL SCHOOL

Dale Harmon Barnhart
Bonnie Beck
Kenneth D. Benson
Robert Blue
Keith Eugene Brown
Harold Clausen
James Conway
Patricia Ann Cumming
Florence Ruth Dumke
Carrol Engebretson
Robert Fletcher Erickson
Arthur Lloyd Getting
Preston Hippen
Donald Krenos
Florence Lyng
John Richard Michael
Graham Nolan Orth
Dona L. Overgaard
Doris Mae Overgaard
Dona Mae Palmer
Beverly Mavis Schmidt
Artha-Jane Shipton
Robert Souter
Douglas Sugrue
Phyllis Thompson
Myron L. Weiss

Robert J. Huhn
Robert B. Jolivette
Joseph Allen Klock
Joyce D. West
Bernice May Whaler
Marilyn Adele Youngren

## LONGFELLOW SCHOOL

Paul Arnopoulos
Theodore Beuckens
Leonard M. Blackburn
Joanne Dedrick
Darold E. Fredricks
Ruth Howalt
Walter Carlton Leyse
William Lowe
Kenneth Malloy
John McLaughlin
James McLaughlin
Marlene Michael
Harry Mitchell
Donald Modica
Richard Neisch
William Onnenga
Shirley Paul
LaVon Polzien
Ronald Richardson
Ronald Ryan
Charles Simpson
Marcella Tripp
James Tyler
Gerald Warren
D. William Zaayer

## MARK TWAIN SCHOOL

Elver B. Atwood
Betty Lavon Ball
Carol Victoria Berg
Harry L. Bogdos
Frederick D. Clements
Myren A. Daggett
Charles Ronald Decker
Donald E. Fairbanks
Hazel V. Green
Donna Mae Hansen
Joy Corbett McCord
Wayne M. Mortrude
Robert Willis Naylor
Mary Louise Nelson
Constance Jeanne Rossman
Velda Marilyn Severson
Dolores A. Whitcomb
Mary Marlene Williams

## WHITTIER SCHOOL

Roger F. Bakke
Harry M. Bartunek
Laura Delphine Canfield
Geraldine Mae Chipperfield
Dio Lewis Coffield
Esther Arlene Drossel
Ervin C. Fields
Delores M. Fisher
Jeanne Ann Frahm
Donald L. Freese
LeRoy M. Gould
Richard Guenther
William Haley
Audrey Hamilton
Bidea Hamway
Merwin Hanten
Helen L. Hargus
Donald Wayne Harmer
Lowell J. Harmer
Verner E. Hartmann
Charles Eugene Hibbison
Lawrence Holm
Julius Jacobson, Jr.
La Rae Jensen
Violet Jensen
Jacqueline Frances Jewell
Beverly Ruth Johnson
Delores Lillian Johnson
Myrtle G. Johnson
Beverly Darlene Jurgensen
Charlotte Therese Kolb
Penzill L. Lane
Mary Jean Lentz
Donald Lilyquist
Virgil Eugene McMaster
Richard D. Michael
Roger Wayne Nagel
Lucille Nelson
James B. Ogdie
James Page
Carol Frances Reaves
Janet Beverly Rensberger
Joan Evelyn Rensberger
Donald William Schmeyer
Bonnie Rae Smith
Shirlee Frances Smith
Dolores D. Spindler
Donald Stansbury
Helen Jean Story
Frank Straw
Jeanette Marie Sylliaasen
Donald LeRoy Taylor
Beverly Jean Thomas
Lois Mae Thompson
Donna Mae Thoreson
Brenton Dewaine Tilden
David Van Diepen
James Dewey Wenbourne
George Wyant

*The house on Madison Street in West Sioux was a haven for reading and reflection for me in the late '40s, except during an occasional flooding. (Charles Fredricks)*

*West Sioux Falls, looking east on West Madison Street, during the 1951 or 1952 flood. The Fredricks' house is to the right of the center. (Charles Fredricks)*

# 22
# West Sioux Falls Experience

When I was 15 years old, a move to 1720 West Madison Avenue was necessary. My sister and her husband, Vern, had moved out of town. She and her husband had been taking care of the family. My bother-in-law had taken a job in western South Dakota on a road-construction crew. The years at Fifteenth and Elmwood had been too short a time to develop strong relationships as Third Avenue had and this move was easier. The move was not looked upon as a big change in my life as the ties of friends at Washington High School remained strong and a bond in my life.

Too many outside activities had been occupying my head. Work at the Sport Bowl and studies in High School had widened my world extensively. I had acquired many more buddies and acquaintances beyond my immediate family and they occupied my life now.

Little did I realize that the move to West Sioux was to add another dimension to my life that would change my outlook forever.

The small one-story, two-bedroom, brown-shingled house at 1720 Madison Street was well isolated from the rest of the community. Down the dirt road to the west about five blocks was Brockhouse's Grocery Store and a number of small businesses that comprised the center of West Sioux. One block to the east there stood the abandoned hospital barracks of the Army Radio Training Base, remnants of the just completed war. They would be pressed into use as an elementary school in a couple of years, as West Sioux was increasing its population rapidly. The fence to the base had been knocked down and part of the black-topped army road was being used as a short cut to Burnside. This shortcut to downtown saved a longer route around Elmwood and then east on Burnside. Later North Western Avenue would be built here, the barracks removed and business encouraged to use the area as a business park. The future of the area surrounding my home would be designated for use as a recreation complex in the late 1950s and its isolation violated. McCart Park was developed to the south and after razing the house I lived in, a city complex of offices was built in the 1990s. In the 1940s there was no sewer, city water or paved roads at this dead-ended Madison Avenue. An 'outhouse' was a necessity, and a hand-worked water pump the only means of getting water. Eventually a sewer line was blasted through the quartzite rock that underlay the area and exposed itself in many places. Further to the west of the Sioux River, this rock was being quarried for use as a building material. Water was supplied to the house by a large metal hand pump that stood a yard high and needed two hands for most to work. This pump was set in the floor of a small lean-to shed attached to the back of the house. The back door of the house led into this shed and another door exited. A kitchen was just inside the back door and it had a refrigerator, table, and a three-burner kerosene stove used for cooking. Farmers' matches were needed to light the wick of the stove after it was soaked wet with kerosene, a sometimes long process to get the stove going. There was a single naked electric bulb hanging from the ceiling that provided the only light after dark.

A standing kerosene heater was used in the adjoining front room that had two bedrooms off from it. The bedrooms did not benefit from the small heater in the frontroom and were exceedingly cold in the wintertime.

One of the bedrooms was used by my sister, June, for the few months before she got married and left the house. The other bedroom was mine. It was a cheerful room with windows on the east and north street side. I had never had a bedroom to myself before and I thoroughly enjoyed sleeping alone in the room. The walls eventually became plastered with photographs, magazine articles, and newspaper articles pertaining to the events at Washington High School. These mementoes became my focus during the many hours spent alone in the house.

I enjoyed another first: the house had a yard with a lawn. Or rather almost a quarter section of lawn. It was big and it surrounded three sides of the house. Many hours of pleasure was spent mowing and caring for this newly found jewel in my life. The place felt almost like an estate to me and I enjoyed the grand feeling of spaciousness that it offered.

In addition to the lawn, the unscreened, wooden front porch afforded an unlimited opportunity to indulge myself in an increasingly favorite pastime. The wide vista view from the front porch had a complete sweep of all the fields to the right and left with the green grass of a golf driving range spread out across the dirt street to the south. I could see all the way to the Starlite Drive In on Burnside. At night it was quite a spectacular view that produced hours of day-dreaming pleasure as I sat at night watching from the front porch.

In 1948 I discovered how much a book can be a comfort and a friend. I was 15 years old and I was living at 1720 Madison Avenue. The house sat in the midst of a large, green lawn with a large Elm tree close to the road in front. The huge, tall Elm tree offered a great comfort of shade when the sun beat down in the summer.

The first summer at this house I was alone most of the time as my sister, who was still unmarried, was working long hours at Skinlo's Cafe on west Twelfth Street. My dad was out of town working much of the time so I took care of the house, mowed the lawn, and tried to keep busy so I wouldn't go stir-crazy.

*From my front porch I spent summer evenings watching the activity at the West Sioux Starlite Drive In Theater. (Charles Fredricks)*

The summer in South Dakota can be long for a fifteen year old when he has nothing to do and it took me a couple of weeks to realize that I had to do something with my mind in the heat of the day when he could not work outside. And it had to cost nothing. It was during one of these lulls in the afternoon that I remembered that the library was open in the summer as well as during the school year. The next day I walked down to the City Library on Tenth and Dakota and reintroduced myself to the varied wonders that were on the bookshelves of the library. I checked out Jules Verne's *Journey to the Center of the Earth.* I couldn't wait until I got home to find out what it was about. Who goes to the center of the earth? It's impossible, right? Probably just a lot of nonsense. I was wrong. The writing and adventure that he presented was fascinating. I was in the center of the earth with him. I couldn't set the book down. These few hours spent reading Jules Verne were the greatest and most exhilarating hours I had spent so far this summer. It was great. I wanted to read more. I couldn't wait to get back to the library and check out another book to read.

I took out two books next time. It was something about traveling across the United States, and one about hunting for treasure in the oceans. People could actually hunt under the ocean with suits on that had oxygen pumped into them so they wouldn't drown. Terribly close to danger all of the time, I thought. Wet and cold, but it might be fun. The next book I checked out was a thick, 1000-page book called Anthony Adverse. It was slow reading, but it was fascinating. As a young boy, he, Anthony Adverse, had climbed trees and looked over the city the same as I had done. He seemed real to me. It was a long book, but I persevered until I finally traveled to an exotic place called Timbuktu—a place in Africa. Anthony had traveled far, made a success of his life and accumulated a fortune. It was a great adventure. Before the summer was over, I had read dozens of books from the library and I had developed a greater appreciation of reading than I ever thought possible. Books had become an intimate part of my existence. The habit of reading that I had developed that summer stayed with me. I continued reading every type of book throughout my entire life.

*Saturday night is the loneliest night of the week..........*

*The Sioux Falls Public Schools Central Services complex now occupies my former home site on West Madison Street. (FF collection)*

# 23
# Montana Summer

Uncle Bill moved to Sheridan, Wyoming in the late '40s and after a summer job at Girton Adams Ice Company, I hitchhiked to Sheridan,Wyoming. I actually had been fired from the job after my boss found out I was only fifteen years old. I had successfully passed myself off as an eighteen year old while I was at Girton Adams. Now would be a good time to go see uncle Bill, my sister Nancy and my relatives who were raising her. Although hitchhikers were always looked upon with suspicion, it was a good way to travel. Also it was a potentially great adventure that made me try this trip.

The second 'hitch' was great. It was a salesman driver from Sioux Falls. This ride resulted in a lifelong friendship. The salesman bought me lunch and gave me good conversation from Chamberlain where he picked me up. The ride lasted all the way into Rapid City. The first night I spent at the Harney Hotel in a 50 cent bed in the basement. Finding a hotel accommodation and sleeping in a hotel for the first time was a new experience. Next morning I was back on the road. After a half-hour of frustration I started realizing that it was going to be a more difficult job hitchhiking through the Black Hills. A few three and four mile rides finally got me past Mt. Rushmore and to Custer, but the rides were few and far between. Custer to Newcastle went fast with one good ride, then I had a long wait. The cars that came were few and far between so I enjoyed the surrounding scenery. The next ride was strange. The older man didn't say much and drove looking straight ahead only with no conversation between us. Finally he apologized by saying this was as far as he could take me and the pickup turned off a side road and stopped.

I got out.

Where the hell was I? In the middle of nowhere, I thought. The pickup continued down the side road trailing a cloud of dust and as I looked around at the junction I saw only a small dilapidated house across the highway.

The road was deserted for miles both east and west. I was more concerned with the cars coming from the east but if there was no luck thumbing that way I knew that Newcastle was to the east and if all else failed I could go back that way. All of these choices kept going through my head with decisions being made in favor of each choice but it didn't make any difference what decision I made, there hadn't been a car pass in front of me for an entire hour.

Finally I heard the faint sound of a car coming from the east so I checked my thumb and my pack to make sure that both were ready to move.

ZOOM—the car zipped by without even a honk from the horn.

More waiting. The sky was clear without a cloud in it. There were absolutely no sounds being made around the area. It was extremely quiet and it lent itself to a lot of thinking and wondering time. With no one to talk to, a person can sure make up a lot of queer conversations with himself.

More waiting.

Another half-hour passed and by now I had put myself into a very subdued, thoughtful state.

The sun was moving fast toward the west. Late afternoon had arrived. Again I heard the approach of another car from the east. It came into view about three miles away and I stood up straight beside the road in anxious anticipation with my hand bag beside me at me feet.

As it got within a mile, I put out my arm straight as I could and pointed my thumb slightly upward.

It worked. The car was stopping.

I was overjoyed at the prospect of a ride. Gillette. Great. I thanked him as I got into the car and began down the road. At Gillett I bid goodbye and stepped out with my little traveling bag. It was really getting late as I walked toward the edge of town to continue hitchhiking. After a half-hour of waiting and looking around I decided to chuck hitchhiking for the day and go find the Greyhound Bus Depot. The rest of the way was to be spent in the comfort of the bus as I bought a ticket on the 9:30 PM bus to Sheridan.

The bus was late. While riding the bus, in a drowsy half-asleep mood I remembered stopping at a little gas station at Spotted Horse for a passenger to get off. Then I drifted into another sleep stupor for the rest of the bumpy ride.

The bus rolled into Sheridan. As I searched for my Uncle Bill's address I became panic. I had lost it. I immediately started figuring out what I had to do to find Uncle Bill. It was a small town he lived in so it shouldn't cause much of a problem, I thought. Trouble. The phone book didn't give me the information I wanted so I took a walk around the main street to give myself time to think. During my walk I spotted the police station. There were lights on inside of. As I stood there, I started shivering. I wasn't dressed for the cool mountain nights around here. After some quick deliberation, I decided I had to get out of the cool night air, fast, as I was shaking now. The policemen in the station might could help me. Like most midwesterners I had always avoided policemen as much as possible until last resorts necessitated it. This was a difficult situation and it called for hard decisions. Swallowing my pride and apprehension was hard to do.

The two officers behind the desk looked me over with suspicion as I entered the police station, but they were extremely nice as I explained my problem. They immediately decided to look through the telephone book as I had done, hoping that I may have missed the name. They had no luck either. "Probably will be tax records at the courthouse," one of they offered, but the courthouse doesn't open until morning, they informed me. It was getting close to 2:00 AM by now and after a small conference by the policemen they offered to let me sleep the rest of the night in one of the jail cells until the courthouse opened in the morning. I wouldn't have thought of that idea. I had never been inside a jail cell, let alone sleeping in one. I had seen gangster movies and I felt I knew what to expect from these movie experiences. I was totally scared. It didn't comfort me much when the policeman said the cell I could sleep in was in the women's section of the jail. But they comforted me by saying that there were no prisoners in the cell that night.

The policeman led me into the cell with one bed and a blanket on it.

"Goodnight," he said, and left the door open as he left. I stood there. The room was cold, but I was afraid to close the open window. I checked the cell door again to make sure it was open, then I lay down on top of the bed with my clothes on. I lay shivering in the cool mountain air but I decided that I wasn't going to get under the covers. It would be more difficult to get out of the cell if somebody sneaked back and locked the door, I told myself.

I was terrified. It was a jail. Don't let them lock the door, I told myself. I'll stay awake and make sure they don't come back. Finally my eyes grew too heavy. Eventually in spite of the cool air, I fell asleep.

The morning came none too soon. I felt punchy. The little sleep I had gotten made me half-groggy. I almost ran out of the jail after saying 'goodby' to the jailers.

The warm morning sun felt good after the cold night. County courthouses have a multitude of records on the citizens of the communities they serve and it didn't take long to locate the address of my cousin Jack's auto business but we could not find any address for my Uncle Bill.

After getting direction from the county clerk to the auto repair shop I started walking in the direction of his business looking over every store on the way. Before long I found myself standing at a vacant corner lot in disbelief. I thought that I had the directions to the shop correctly written down. I looked them over again. Suddenly from behind me I heard—"What do you want here?" in a gruffy voice. I spun around. There was Uncle Bill standing there with a big sheepish-grin on his face.

"What the hell! Where did you come from?" I shouted with joy.

"I recognized you as you passed the shop a block back and I started following you."

"Damn it. The clerk gave me the wrong directions. How are you? Where's Alt at? How is she?"

There was a good reason that I hadn't found Uncle Bill's address in the phone book: he had moved across the state line into Montana. He had leased a ranch outside Decker, Montana, not too far from the Little Big Horn Custer Battlefield National Monument. It was just a stroke of luck that I had caught him in town. He had come in for groceries and a shave. He hated shaving with his straight razor as he cut himself too much so he would let his beard grow all week and then go to the barber in town. Our cousin Jack had a garage in Sheridan and Bill had just stopped by to get a cup of coffee and some conversation before going to the barber. Great bit of luck that he had spotted me going by. It was a great relief to find him.

In 1948, Decker, Montana, 12 miles north of Sheridan, Wyoming, was a spot in the road on the Montana-Wyoming border. The Tongue River flowed east of the town that is not too far from the Little Big Horn river to the west. Eventually a dam was built on the tongue River to create a reservoir for irrigation in the sun-parched country. It was smack in the middle of nowhere with hardly anyone around except a few ranchers. The area is very isolated with few roads.

Uncle Bill, his wife Alt, and I left in his jeep for this outpost of civilization that afternoon. Groceries for the week had been purchased in Sheridan. This trip to town afforded the only opportunity to see people other than each other and to buy groceries. Following the dirt road to Decker in the open jeep was an adventure in itself. We stopped at a small general store halfway to the turnoff to the ranch. At the store Bill talked for a bit as only Bill could do and then he bought a box of .22 bullets.

"What do you need 500 bullets for?" I asked him.

"You'll see," was his reply.

I wasn't sure why he hadn't purchased the shells in town, but I realized later that this was the way people in the West kept in contact with other people. A seemingly simple purchase of supplies at a number of businesses kept you informed of the news of the area and it let the people know what you were doing and that you were all right. It was more of a social contact than a business contact at the store. He may be needed for some type of help in a future emergency and the good-will purchase was justified.

Bill's ranch was a step into the wild, wild West. A kid's dream. Paradise was about to unfold before my eyes and I was to begin to experience the best two weeks of my entire lifetime. There was no refrigerator, radio, kitchen appliance, or electric motor at Bill's ranch, as it lacked electricity. It was very quiet at the ranch. He and his wife lived in a one-story stone-walled ranch house that sat on a flat area in the middle of a small lawn. There was a tall cliff to the north of the house and an outhouse and a small creek ran beside the house to the south of it. The creek then ran through a 'spring house' that cooled the milk that was collected from the two cows he milked. A two-story barn set to the east of the house in a hollow about fifty yards away where he kept the two cows and a horse.

Sagebrush was everywhere. As Bill turned off the main road to the town of Decker, he stopped.

"Get out and open the gate," he commanded. I got out of the jeep and opened the barbed wire gate that kept cattle from straying away from the ranch range. After the jeep passed the gate it had to be shut by putting a post that had the wire stapled to it in a wire loop at the bottom of another post, then leveraging the gate past to hook the top of it into another wire loop. For a kid this maneuver can be tricky and hard to do.

It was a couple of miles at 15 miles per hour on a dirt road to the ranch house. All this time I sat wide-eyed looking at every piece of vegetation and hills in sight. What a world to explore.

Days passed fast, and I explored everything.

The thousand or so acres of range held surprise after surprise for me. When Bill said he needed coal for the stove and handed me a bucket I stood puzzled. I hadn't seen any coal pile around the house or barn and I didn't know where he wanted me to get some. 'Go dig it up' he said and I really felt he was putting me on again. He wasn't, though. We got into the jeep with a shovel and pick and drove a few hundred feet around the cliff by the house. There we found a seam of coal in the side of the mountain and we picked and shoveled a load of coal into the jeep. This area of Montana and Wyoming had been the bottom of a huge lake when the coal was formed. Vegetation accumulated on the bottom of the lake and eventually it was compressed into coal. When the pioneers landed on the eastern sea coast, hard coal was discovered in the Appalachian Mountains and it was exploited by digging tunnels to get it. A lot of environmental damage occurred as well as loss of life in this process, but the industrialization of America developed because of this coal. Only later were the coal fields of Montana and Wyoming discovered, but they were not exploited by drag-line operations until after the Arab Oil embargo in 1973. The drag-line method removes the overburden of land that has accumulated above the coal seam and then big scoops of coal can be removed without the use of mine shafts. It is safer for the miners this way and more efficient. Its fun to speculate what the course of America's development would have been if this enormous supply of coal had been discovered and developed earlier in North American history.

Nights were especially interesting, eerie, and sometimes frightening on the ranch. The yellowish kerosene light was difficult to read or sew by and the light presented weird shadows on the wall. An occasional coyote howl would startle me and Bill eased my anxious state by getting his 30-30 rifle.

He poked it out of the door and fired off a round into the air. "That'll take care of them until morning," he said looking at his wife, Alt, and winking. A while later the coyote howled again. No one noticed but me.

The day was hot and uncomfortable for me.

"Want to make some ice cream, Fred?" Bill asked.

What is he talking about now? He knew that ice was needed to make ice cream and he also knew there was no refrigeration to make the ice here. I told him so, but he only laughed. Leading me to the jeep, he proceeded to drive toward the main road but he turned north half-way there. A small dirt road, actually more of a trail, led to a number of barns and a house after a half-hour of driving. "Nobody here now," he said as he looked around and started toward the barn. Inside the barn he started kicking the barn floor before I noticed that he was kicking the sawdust away from the bottom of the floor. He cleared a spot in the sawdust with his feet. All of a sudden I saw a large block of ice beneath the cleared space in the sawdust. "Help me," he said as he got on his knees and put his hand between a crack in the ice. We lifted a huge chunk of ice and it was then that I realized that it was river ice. The rancher living here last winter had cut a number of blocks of ice from the river and stored it below the barn floor and then he covered it with sawdust to keep it from melting. Another pioneer lesson learned.

The ice cream we made that afternoon using the river ice was delicious.

The greatest adventure of my life was yet to come. After five days of exploring the immediate ranch area and having climbed the hill to the north a few times, the city boy in me grew tired of this and I ached for more excitement.

Glancing at me first, Bill took out his .22 six-shooter one day from a drawer where he kept it. It was in a leather holster with a number of bullets in the belt holder. My eyes bugged out. I had target practiced with a single shot .22 rifle and I had hunted a few times but never with a pistol. It held a great deal of fascination for me. "Come on Fred, lets go for a ride."

Ten minutes in the jeep brought us to an area where a lot of tin cans and discarded equipment lay on the ground. This was the area the ranchers had used as a dumpsite. Everything was left to rust on top of the ground. We got out and Bill strapped the holster on his hip and walked toward the dump. There he set up a number of tin cans and a few bottles upright on the ground and then he stepped away from them. Taking careful aim he began shooting at the targets. All of the time I was really getting excited to try my skill and show Bill what I could do. Finally I got my chance. Bill watched and jeered me when I missed a target but I could see that he was pleased that I knew how to safely fire the pistol. Finally Bill unbuckled the holster and handed it to me along with the pistol and the box of shells.

After returning to the ranch Bill saddled up the old gray horse he kept in the barn and told me to go enjoy myself.

"You mean by myself?"

"Yes, go, anywhere you want. But don't do anything foolish. Keep that pistol pointed away from you and the horse." He walked back to the house leaving me alone.

Oh my god! As I reined the horse and headed toward the dirt road my head was spinning. What a feeling. I was experiencing the greatest feeling of joy that a fifteen-year-old thought imaginable. Alone, with a horse and a pistol. What do I do first? Is it really true? The open range was before me, a good saddle horse was beneath me, and my six-shooter was at my hip. Watch out tin cans and bottles! I shot at everything I could find. I shot at cans and bottles from on the horse, off the horse, lying down, standing up, and from between my legs. Old Paint and I explored every gully and hill on the entire ranch and then some.

Within a few days my ammunition to kill tin cans ran out and I carried only an empty six-shooter now. Very degrading for a city slicker. By this time only a few more days were left before I had to pack my duffel bag and return to Sioux Falls, civilization, and another year of high school. This had been the most memorable summer imaginable and it was not soon forgotten.

*Irene, goodnight Irene, I'll see you in my dreams.........*

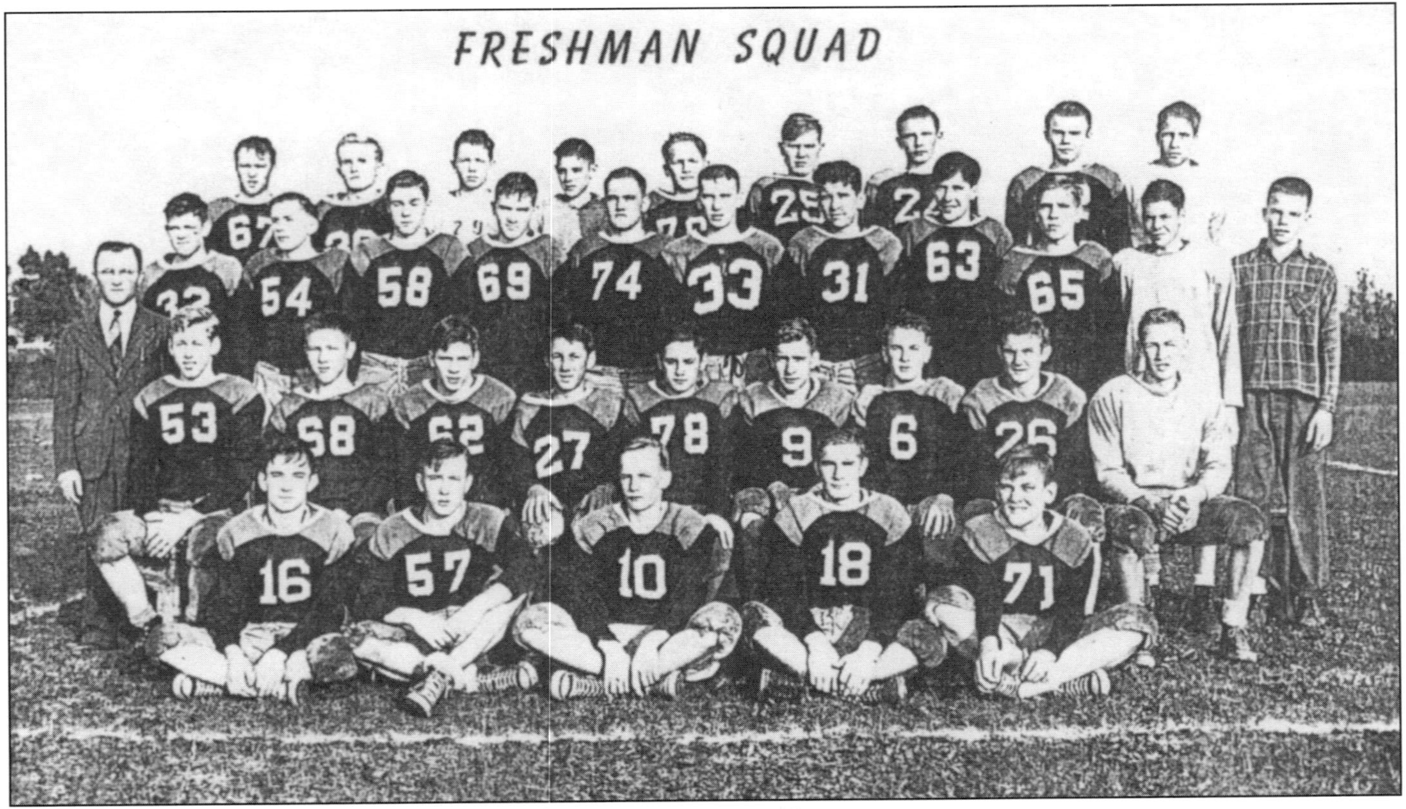


**1947 Freshmen Football Team.**

*Back row, left to right: Guenther, Oistad, West, Teslow, Hanson, Rowland, Reppe, Wylie, and Bowen. Third row: Mortrude, Larson, Erickson, Beatty, Donaldson, Howes, Liliquest, Greenslate, Kraft, Bartholow, and Norberg. Second row: Coach Kleinsasser, Walton, Reid, Modica, Houck, Kelly, Nelson, Cline, Meyer, and Noel. First row: Decker, Kolb, Simpson, Fredericks, and Enright.*

# 24

# Washington High School Football

My adjustment to high school had been smooth: that was, until I entered P. E. class. I felt I was in my element in the competition of sports. I had always had better than average coordination that had helped me stand out. And I was maturing faster than the other boys. My body had filled out, I was taller than the other boys, and I liked to compete. I excelled at competition. Competition of all types excited me and I always wanted to be on top of the situation. But I was vocal. Almost too vocal. As the year progressed, the Boys' P.E. teacher started getting on my back and demanding that I not be so vocal in competitive games. I could be competitive but not vocal. This attitude of the coach perplexed and galled me. Hell, I was only expressing myself verbally as my playmates and I in the Galesburg area had always done. That was our nature. It was the way we had learned to keep the lid on our physical aggressiveness. Vocalizing was our outlet for some of our aggression. In the Galesburg we didn't use 'bad' language—it was 'our' language. Slowly it began to dawn on me that the area where I had grown up was considered a 'rough' and uncouth area by many of the citizens of the city. The Galesburg kids were different. We lived on the "wrong side of the railroad tracks". Differences were becoming more apparent now that I was in the melting pot of the city. Finally the grades came out. A 'D' grade was given to me in P.E. I knew it was for aggressive attitude and demeanor. The 'D' grade that I had received in P.E. wasn't a comment on my athletic ability but it was a social comment on my behavior. The 'D' grade that I had received in P.E. wasn't a comment on my athletic ability, but it was a social comment on my behavior. I didn't take this lesson lightly.

I was encouraged by many of my friends to go out for football to 'show them' what the boys from Galesburg had. As a freshman I couldn't compete on the varsity team, but we did play against the 'big boys' in scrimmage. The freshman team showed the coaches a great deal of potential. Led by the likes of boys like Bob Walton, Darrell Erickson, and Dick Merrill, and me, the varsity coach was amazed when the upstart freshmen gave an outstanding accounting against the bigger boys.

Washington High School had over two-thousand students in the late 1940s. Although it was the biggest high school in the five surrounding states of North and South Dakota, Wyoming, Nebraska, and Minnesota, its record in varsity football had been only average in the last few years. The school had more athletics than any other school that they played but it was evident that something was wrong with their football players. Their potential was not being utilized. To top it all off, the student body expressed its displeasure and lack of support in no uncertain way. Principal Beck constantly pleaded with the student body to attend the games and after attending to please stay until the contests were over. Leaving was not polite, he admonished. The football team continued to play poorly.

The morale builder of all times was uttered by the coach after the usual disastrous year. 'You can't win them all' the coach would tell the players after losing another contest. This did nothing for their pride and they wanted to at least win against Cathedral High School, a feat that hadn't happened enough times.

I could not compete my sophomore year. When the physicals were given, I found that I had a hernia. That devastated me. But I made a good thing out of a bad situation by using the year lifting weights at the YMCA even though I had a medical problem. It turned out to be a grand year in spite of missing football season.

I was ready for my junior year of football, but in 1949 the football coaching situation changed. A new football coach from Yankton was hired. This coach came to WHS with high recommendations and accomplishments. He had played at South Dakota State on championship teams and after a stint in the service he developed an excellent football team at Yankton High School. His name was Bob Burns and his reputation of toughness and excellent coaching had impressed the school trustees enough that they wanted him to coach the Warriors. The first meeting with the football squad was a memorable event. The football candidates trying out for the team lined up for their equipment in the locker room at Howard Wood Field on Tenth and Franklin. His first appearance was deceptive. He didn't look anything like a championship coach. First of all he was too short, and he looked like a fireplug. He had beady eyes, and he appeared to foam at the mouth slightly when he talked excitedly. Pacing up and down the field house like a coyote in a cage, he never stopped asking questions of the players lined up getting their football gear. He was never still. He roamed the room constantly, unable to sit still.

'What do you weigh?' 'Did you go out for track last spring?' 'What position did you play last year?' 'You've got big hands, can you catch a ball?' 'How tall are you?' etc.. etc., etc. Each boy who was grilled answered briskly. The attitude of the coach excited us. His 'no nonsense' attitude and concern made us stand up straighter and think harder. The old coach wasn't this way. This new coach gave the impression that he meant business. His command of football became immediately known to us when the practice sessions began.

I went about my business of putting on my football gear. My leather helmet didn't fit and I exchanged it for a larger one. Pants and pads were put on. 'Tough Skin' was swabbed on the ankles and then they were taped. The practice jersey was put over my shoulder pads. I felt like a warrior with all of the gear on. It felt terrific.

Then the practices began. Calisthenics—over a half-hour of them. Jumping jacks to warm up, then bend and touch the ground with your fingers, next push-ups, leg lifts until you felt like dying. The two-a-day workouts became nightmares to us. The prevailing attitude at that time was that workouts were meant to be rough and tough and conditioning meant that no water was to be allowed on the field. No water! The sun was boiling us to death and yet no water intake was allowed until the end of the practice. Needless to say a number of players fell by the wayside and quit after suffering the 'dry heaves'... but not me. I knew I could survive to play. I needed to survive and play football. The demands on my body and will that football offered was like a dream come true. Here I could demonstrate all of my athletic skill and at the same time release my pent-up frustration and antagonism that I felt society had heaped upon me. This socially-accepted outlet for my frustration was exactly what was needed to let off the steam from my boilers. I could hit, punch, and knock over people and obstacles at will, under the rules of course, and still be praised for this behavior. I adjusted and developed rapidly to this new type of activity. And they praised me for it. What more could be asked of a sport?

..............................

As the season opened high expectation prevailed in the players. The new, multiple offenses that Coach Burns was trying to use was complicated and hard to learn. Strong right, T-formation left, thirty-six around end, etc. Drill, drill, drill. That's all the players did. Slowly we began to execute the plays fairly well. However, too many thought that the new coach ensured success regardless of the players ability. Lessons were to be learned by experience. Confidence in members of the team was extremely high. Everyone agreed that we were winners even before the season began. The attitude was that the season was to be a triumph beyond their wildest dreams. But the reality of life was about to jolt many of the players.

The days were cooler now that the school and football season had begun. Practice was now after school at Howard Wood Field on East Tenth Street and it was now over two hours long. Most of the players had to walk to the stadium from Washington High School although a few fortunate ones hitched rides with their buddies that had a car. These were mainly seniors. During my junior year I walked to the practice sessions, then I walked home to West Sioux after the practice session. The energy I burned up was enormous. I was always hungry.

Then the regular season contests began. The first game was with cross-town rival Cathedral High School. It turned out to be a disaster. The game had all the elements associated with traditional cross-town rivalry. For days all of the conversation in the city focused on this 'big' game. Washington High School could not lose, everyone agreed. All of the players wanted to win in the worst way. When the game was over, WHS had lost. The first game against cross-town rival Cathedral knocked this cocky attitude out of their minds as the Burns team lost 19 to 7. This was humiliating. I did not play in the contest. I was on the second-string behind Tom Amburn.

The next game was to be played at Brookings. The team had to travel by bus to the stadium. It was a classic fall evening and great for football- cool, but not cold. The game ended with the Burns men coming out on top with a 13 to 0 win over Brookings. Finally a good win. It was exciting, and exactly what the new coaches, Burns and Heckenlively, had needed. They felt that the team had 'jelled' and that they were now going to be the biggest winners in the Eastern South Dakota Conference. I played in the game for a few short minutes. After the game we showered and packed our gear in our duffel bags to be put on the bus for the return trip. After everybody was on the bus, the driver slowly drove out of the stadium grounds. Coach Burns stood by the driver talking to him and the driver kept shaking his head in the affirmative. I had noticed the route we had taken to the stadium but now we were returning by a different route. As the bus approached the downtown the driver pulled into the front of a large building and stopped. Immediately this got the attention of the players.

"Why were we stopping here?" I asked.

"Got to eat," one of the seniors blurted out, as if the younger players were total geeks.

"Eat? I don't have any money with me to buy food." I thought to myself. We never ate after the games in Sioux Falls, I continued thinking to myself. I can get by until I get home.

By now the players were moving out of the bus and into the restaurant. I followed cautiously and reluctantly. The place looked too ritzy for me. I had never been in a restaurant that looked this fancy. My heart beat faster as I walked into the restaurant and I felt panicky. I knew I wouldn't be able to pay for a meal here. I had no money. It was too expensive.

Trailing the rest of the group, I followed them into a large banquet hall. It was massive! I had never seen a table as large as this. The table was already set with shiny silverware and over forty plates. Did they know we were coming? I wondered. Waiters were bringing in salads and placing them beside the plates. It looked inviting and my stomach began churning with hunger pains. The players who had entered first were already in the process of setting down, and the mood of the group was very happy.

Hesitatingly I moved to the table and took a chair beside one of the second-string players whom I had sat next to on the bench during the game that night.

"Sit down Fred," he called to me. "Time to eat."

I rarely spoke to most of the players about personal matters and feelings but I felt compelled to at this time.

"I can't pay for a meal here." I said to him, half-embarrassed.

"Don't worry. You don't pay. After every away game, we get a meal. It's a long ride back to Sioux Falls, and we'll get back late, so they have to buy us a meal," he confided in me.

A meal! A free meal? I couldn't believe it. And what a meal it was. Salad, with dressing. Bread—rolls. Potatoes, gravy, and a steak. A steak! Man, this is living. A great big steak for myself.

During my football career at Washington High School, I looked forward to the games we played away from Sioux Falls. I always got a banquet, a reward I grew to cherish with every game.

Brookings fell to WHS by a score of 13 to 0. This was a short-lived habit of victory because in the next games against Yankton, East, Central, and Aberdeen we lost. WHS reverted to its old ways of losing. The school and the town again lost faith in the team.

"You can win, you're better than you've been showing me and the fans." Coach Burns exhorted in his raspy voice that had been become horse by his continual side-line yelling for perfection in execution of plays that went awry.

Orange Letter Day proved to be the turning point for WHS in 1949. Heavily-favored, unbeaten Rapid City came to town and we defeated them after a hard-fought battle. The team was ecstatic. Burns was pleased. Now things would be different, I thought to myself. Although I had not played in the game, I felt I was part of the victory by just being on the team.

The final two teams we played—Mitchell and Watertown—were defeated. The faith came back. But Coach Burns had never lost faith in us, or his system. This attitude was the team's salvation. However, the word went out at the end of the season: there would be few monogram letters given out this year. Coach Burns felt that the letters were given out too freely in the past season. I didn't receive a monogram letter. That hurt.

..............................

My muscles bulged underneath the undersized white T-shirt that proclaimed 'Warriors' on it. The many months of body building at the YMCA were beginning to pay off for me. "Quit that weightlifting" the football coach had warned, "it'll make you muscle bound and too slow for the team next year. I need a fast, quick, pulling guard, not a muscle-bound slow dunce," he said. These words didn't penetrate my mind or make me stop lifting. The three hours of workout at the "Y" gym on Monday, Wednesday, and Friday were looked forward to with a great deal of satisfaction. My large frame with the light blond hair forming on my chest responded favorably to the workouts. I had taken to it with the dedication of a divinity student. I had finally found something that I really liked and it satisfied me. As the muscles increasingly responded, the intensity of the workouts increased. I challenged myself to the utmost. Never had I felt so in command of myself and the universe. Weightlifting produced a fabulous feeling of accomplishment and my self-esteem soared. Nothing like this had happened before to me. I was now addicted to the workouts.

I noticed my female typing teacher started making sly remarks about my big broad shoulders as she slightly caressed them embarrassingly. Incidents such as this didn't go unnoticed by me and they gave me a slightly aroused, strange feeling even though the teacher was much older than I was.

My posture and physique had started changing noticeably in the last year of grade school. My buddies, Walt, Don, Ted, and Bill seemed to stop growing as I shot upward. They seemed like boys now, and I felt much older. I had a firm 150 pounds plus weight when I entered high school, and my weight continued to increase. The increase in the width of the shoulders made it difficult to find shirts that would fit. They always looked too small. Not able to buy new clothes, the old ones had to wear out by the time I could afford them, but by the time this happened I felt like 'Lil Abner of the comic strips. I was yet to have a pair of low-cut dress shoes and the 'clod hoppers' I wore intensified my masculine appearance. As the body got larger, the clothes didn't seem to matter. I had sensed the older people I knew had started changing. I was being looked upon as more of an adult and the talk to me was more mature. I got along with almost everybody now, but I didn't know why because I felt I was a quite standoffish and isolated from everyone most of the time.

The multi-story Cataract Hotel was at the northwest corner of Ninth and Phillips. Across the street, to the east, was the largest building in South Dakota, a nine-story combination bank and office building. The front had a couple of small windows and a circular sliding door as an entrance to the building. Otherwise, at the street level, the front was blank with large sections of solid block walls.

On a beautiful sunny afternoon, I was walking down Phillips Avenue on my way to the Hollywood Theater to see a movie. I stopped to wait for the green light to cross the Ninth Street intersection. A beautiful blond girl in front of the bank building ahead didn't go unnoticed. While waiting for the light to change I kept her in my view as I nonchalantly glanced around the intersection and up and down Ninth Street. She had noticed me also and she glanced up and down Phillips before looking at me again. As I approached her, she moved slightly away from the building and toward me.

"Hi, how are you?" she asked as I approached her.

"O.K. Nice day isn't it?"

"Yeah, sure, a nice day. You look like you play football, with your big shoulders and everything" (as she touched his arm and ran her hand up to my biceps). "I bet you are on the first team at Washington High School. Right? I used to go with a football player," she continued without stopping to pause.

"Oh. Where?" I asked awkwardly.

"Where? In Iowa where I'm from. He looked a lot like you. I bet you like all of the sports, right?" (She continued again without a pause and still touching my arm she pulled me a little closer to her. I was now touching her body with mine and it felt good). "What you need, she continued, is a magazine that could tell you all about the sports you're interested in. You want to keep on top of everything, don't you," (as she squeezed his biceps). "I happen to have just what you need to keep informed of what's happening all throughout the country. Have you ever heard of Sports Illustrated? Of course you have. Being in sports and everything. All it costs is five dollars. You have five dollars, don't you?"

I slowly put my other hand into my pocket to feel if my money was in that pocket and I nodded 'yes'. (Everything seemed to be happening too fast for my mind—I felt that I was losing control of the situation but it felt so good being next to this beautiful girl that I didn't resist her closeness.)

"If you have five dollars I can order you a subscription to this sports magazine and you'll be getting it in about a month—right to your doorstep. All it costs is five dollars," and she touched my cheek with the back of her hand, actually stroked it.

It was a lot of money, I thought, but I had the money in my pocket.

She pulled out an order form from her purse and had me sign it. All of the time she was talking about Iowa and how I could come and visit her after the football season.

By now I wasn't conscious of anything but the feel of her body close to mine and the sweet smell of her perfume.

"Just give me the five dollars and you'll get the magazine next month."

I gave her a five-dollar bill that I had in my pocket. She took it and started walking toward the corner all of the time talking to me.

"Good-bye," she waved and went around the corner of the building onto Ninth Street and toward the river.

I watched her go around the corner. I then slowly turned and began walking north toward the Hollywood Theater. Suddenly I reeled around—I'd forgotten to get my receipt for the magazine. Hurriedly I ran to the corner where she had turned. She wasn't in sight.

I stood there, feeling perplexed and dumb. It all happened so fast. I just felt dumb. I had lost control. What had happened?

Months passed but no magazine arrived in the mail. After waiting for three months to get my first copy of the sports magazine, I gave up. I knew I had been conned by the girl from Iowa.

..............................

Fall in South Dakota is an exhilarating time of the year. Especially for me.

I always had looked forward to September. Although I wouldn't admit it, even to myself, the return to school was very exciting. I got to meet new friends, renew old acquaintances, and start on a new road to bettering myself.

Also the football season begins. For me this was very important in 1950. I was a senior at WHS. This was to be my last year of high school. I liked school. I enjoyed the challenge of the books, the teachers, and the opportunity to play football. This was to be it. What life would hold for me after leaving WHS was a complete mystery. This was it, the last year, maybe my final opportunity to stand out from the crowd, to make a name for myself, and I had to make as much of it as I could, for I knew this time would never come again.

Most of the summer had been spent working on the docks of the Wilson Trucking Company on Reid and Eighth Street. It was a job Coach Burns had helped me get for the summer, hauling freight around the docks from truck to truck. It had been hard, heavy work and Coach Burns was right, it kept me in shape. It didn't pay very well. I worked 60 hours a week and took home less than 50 dollars. Every other week, I had to work on Sundays (70 hours that week), and still I made less than 60 dollars. From this paycheck I had to buy shoes, clothes, food, put gas in my brother's borrowed car that I used to get to work, and when the week was finished, I barely had enough to save for next year's school clothes. As the summer progressed, I became convinced that I did not want to do this type of physical labor for a living. I was ready and glad to return to school after this hard summer at Wilson's Trucking Company.

The thought of playing football in my senior year was uppermost in my thoughts. This was to be the second coaching season for Coach Bob Burns and Grant Heckenlively. Would they continue to be as impressive this year as they were in their first year when the team finished strong, but didn't win the championship with their four win/five loss season? This was to be the year that the team needed victories to vindicate their lackluster 1949 football record. Would they be able to convince the public that they were not just a flash-in-the-pan? Their reputation was on the line.

When the team members reported for the first day of the fall practice, everyone was extremely enthusiastic and optimistic. The spirit of the returning team members was high. The winning attitude the team had achieved at the end of the 1949 season appeared to be as strong as the day we turned in our football gear last year. The coach hoped that this enthusiasm and spirit would continue throughout the year of 1950. Everyone felt that big things were about to happen. Washington High School was on the edge of greatness.

But I had to prove myself first. In the locker room the first day I found out that the coach had picked Alonzo Smith for the first string tackle. 'No way,' I thought. What makes the coach think Smith is better? First of all he's a junior. And second of all I'm better. I'll just have to prove it to the coach. It was head to head for the first two weeks. Our first game with Madison was coming up. The coach used both Alonzo and me in the practices evenly. Then Alonzo sprained his ankle. I now had the edge. And I never looked back. From that time on, my size, strength, and experience made me the number one choice of the coach for the tackle position.

The first six games were winners for WHS. Madison was the first win: 20 to 7. Our right half-back, Paul Kolb broke his ankle and he was sidelined for the season. This was not, however, a total loss for him as he became elected marshal for Orange Letter Day, an honor he could not have accepted if he had been playing on the football team. In succession we beat Huron 46 to 0, Brookings 20 to 12, Yankton we blanked 46 to 0, beat Sioux City East 26 to 7, Sioux City Central 20 to 12, and Aberdeen 27 to 6. Despite our lop-sided victories, the fans continued to pack the stadium just to see Coach Burns' exciting team.

Ten wins in a row since last year when we beat Rapid City six to zero. Now we were in a position to meet them again but this time on their turf in Rapid City. The game was being touted as the game of the unbeaten titans. Although there was no such thing as a state championship, everyone knew this was it. Rapid City was unbeaten and they were out to avenge their loss of last year. It was to be their homecoming and on top of that, Dad's Day.

They weren't going to let any advantage pass in order to win the game with the highly ranked Washington High School. Our pride was on the line.

The team of thirty players left on Thursday after an all-school rally was held in the auditorium. It was a rousing send-off and we boarded the bus confident we would beat the Cobblers. In Pierre we held a workout at the local school and then the team spent the night at a hotel. Many of the players complained to the coach that they were tired. "Must be the elevation," the coach confided to his assistant, "maybe we should have brought some oxygen with us."

When the Warrior team entered the School of Mines stadium on Friday night, they were met with a horrendous sound of car horns. The Rapid City supporters kept blinking the light of their cars on and off.

"What is this?" I asked the coach.

"They're pulling out all of the stops tonight. The stadium is packed with eight-thousand parents and it's surrounded on three sides with autos. Rapid City is out to beat us tonight. We'll just have to prove them wrong.

During warm-ups, many of the WHS team felt almost sick.

"Has to be the altitude," Coach Burns again confided to his coaches. "We'll have to substitute players early and often," he said. "This may be a long night. I should have brought them here a few days before to get them acclimatized. Too late now though."

Bob Berguin started at center, with Bob Walton, Francis Chase, George Dunham, Jim Unzicker, and Dick Erickson and me filling out the line. Darrell Erickson was the quarterback, backed up by John Peckham, Dwight Hoover, and Kenny Noel. The kickoff went to WHS, but we couldn't get going and we had to give the ball up to Rapid City. They scored on the first play they tried. We were already behind by a score of 7 to 0. My legs didn't respond to my brain. They felt like lead and I could hardly run. Our team was out of it, but we had to hype ourselves up and play. We realized that it was going to be a real struggle to keep up with the Rapid City players. After a fumble by Rapid City, Hoover passed to Erickson to score. The after point was missed. Score 7 to 6. In the second quarter, 'Crazy legs' Thayer of Rapid City led a march to score and after missing the extra point, Rapid City led 13 to 6. Washington High immediately retaliated on the kickoff by scoring on a 65-yard pass from Hoover to Noel. Again the after-point was missed and WHS trailed by 13 to 12. After an exchange of ball possession, the ball was fumbled and Rapid City recovered. They scored and led 20 to 12 at the half-time. We were still in the game but barely when the half-time show began.

The third quarter resulted in a stalemate. Dick Thayer scored in the final quarter and Rapid City led by 27 to 12. After a score by John Peckham,

Hoover scored the extra point and WHS trailed by 27 to 19. A slight glimmer of hope was still open. The final gun sounded with WHS on Rapid City's 25-yard line and driving for a touchdown. It never happened, however.

We sustained a 27 to 19 loss to a very strong Rapid City team. The elevation played a large factor in the loss. Coach Burns had neglected to take into account the thin air and all of the WHS players were wheezing and gulping for air all through the game. Afterwards we all jumped into the Rapid City swimming pool to cool off. It had been a tough season up to this point. The season ended with eight wins, one loss, and one 13 to 13 tie with Watertown at a bone-chilling 13 degree temperature contest.

Washington High School had won the ESD championship. The first time since 1944.

This season was to be the start of a 37-game winning streak by the Orange and Black. WHS had begun a dynasty of success and was to achieve a legend that has been unparalleled in the Heartland.

This year of achieving success as a athlete was the best medicine I could have ever hoped for. I had become a success. The world was not completely against me I now knew. There was hope. I had become a recognized winner.

All of my pain and effort had paid off. Hard work, effort, self-sacrifice, and faith were ideals to live by. The world was my oyster now. At this point in life, I walked taller than I ever thought was possible.

*Onward Sioux Falls, onward Sioux Falls*
*You're the best of all............*

*The YMCA weightlifting program gave me confidence and strength. On the stage of the movie-theater at the Y we held a 'meet' during a Saturday night Teen Canteen in February 1949. (FF Collection)*

***1950 Varsity Football Team***

A-Squad, l. to r., Front row: D. Bowen, S. Pfeifer, D. Hoover, K. Noel, J. Unzicker, J. Nelson, R. Eggiman, J. Skaggs, D. Leach. Second row: D. Paulson, B. Stockstad, B. Berguin, D. Benson, D. Hopewell, G. Dunham, B. Carlson, C. Kemerling, P. Kolb. third row: P. Powell, H. Kirkegaard, D. Wold, F. Cahse, B. Donaldson, J. Peckham, D. Erickson, B. Kraft, D. Bartholow. Fourth row: B. Simpson, A. Smith, H. Neeley, J. Neuroth, J. Kolb, Dick Erickson, B. Walton, D. Merrill, D. Fredricks. *(1951 WHS yearbook)*

# 1950 FOOTBALL REVIEW

THE ORANGE AND BLACK — Friday, November 10, 1950. Page Three

## Sioux Falls Warriors Win ESD Football Championship

### Smoke Signals

LAST WEEK'S PREDICTIONS were correct for a change and I hope I can do as well this week. There are only two games in the ESD conference tonight winding up the football season. The Warriors came back strong in the second half and showed their old style last week and this reporter believes that they should blast Watertown by three touchdowns. The other circuit game should find Mitchell a decisive visitor over Yankton.

CONGRATULATIONS TO ..E football team and Co.. .. for winnin..

### Mitchell Kernels Bow To Conference Champs After Leading Sioux in Rugged First Half

By Bill Larson

Two quarters of football were enough to gain for the Warriors their first ESD pigskin crown since the days of Dworsky. The Warriors thoroughly outclassed the Mitchell Kernels last Friday to come through with a 27 to 7 victory.

**Slow Start**

After a slow, sloppy and an anything but impressive first half, which found the Warriors trailing the purple Kernels 7-6 at intermission, Sioux Falls came alive after a Burns-Heckenlively P... talk. They flew to eleven first downs via the hard-running of P... ..nd Noel and some precision passing by Ike Hooker. F... of th scoring drives were jump passes by "Bi...

### Watertown Meets ESD Champions In Last Game of Season Friday

Watertown is scheduled to meet the new ESD champions, the WHS Warriors, tonight at 8 p. m. at Augustana college field in the final clash of the season.

The Watertown Arrows bowed to Aberdeen 14-0. Earlier in the season they were defeated 28-0 by Rapid City and later they defeated Madison 27-13.

The Arrows have five lettermen from last year's squad. The Watertown probable lineup will be C...mp ar... ..ch at ends, Trandal ... ..s; Dalton a...

W... 'R' S...

Not since the days of Dan Dworsky has a Washington High School eleven championed the E.S.D. Conference. The mighty Warriors of 1950 remained unconquered against all of their conference opponents. Teamwork was the main factor in the Warriors' success. Behind the superb coaching of Burns and Heckenlively, Sioux Falls proved to be the strongest team in the Siouxland as well as in Eastern South Dakota. In the final game of the year, Watertown managed a tie against Sioux Falls, who had previously breezed over all other E.S.D. opponents. In non-conference play the Warriors triumphed over the two Sioux City teams and then met their only defeat at the hands of a strong Rapid City eleven. The season record of eight wins, one tie, and one loss gave the Orange and Black their best season since 1944.

*(1951 WHS yearbook)*

# 25
# Afterthought

In 1940 the population of Sioux Falls was over 40,000 people. The 1950 population had grown to over 52,000 and by 1960 it was to be over 65,000.

The city was bursting at its seams, but the pressure had been alleviated somewhat by the development of new housing starting in the eastern farm fields. This outward development in the Sioux Valley necessitated the development of services that were closer to the developed housing. No longer did the people want to commute through the congestion of the downtown for their living supplies. The roads were congested, the parking was inadequate and aggravated by the advent of revenue-producing parking meters that went against the grain of the conservative customers. They welcomed any business that was nearer to their homes and this decreased the profit of the long-established businesses in the downtown area. A new group of shopping centers were being produced that catered to the new homeowners.

It was a subtle revolution, no big announcements on the radio or the newly-acquired television sets that had become the rage.

No notices in the Argus Leader or the church bulletins.

But the revolution had begun because people were tired being in a mode of forced conservation.

Times no longer demanded saving every scrap of metal to be taken to the scrap pile. Times no longer demanded that you have only one pair of shoes to wear or one suit of clothes to own or demand that everything had to be eaten off the dinner plates that you could now afford. Prosperity was being felt by the entire Heartland finally. No more economic Dust Bowls to contend with.

The time was here for the Heartland to savor the better things of life. New schools for the kids, parks with vast expanses of grass and facilities for baseball fields were being demanded. No longer would the kids have to play in the street.

Up to the beginning of the 1950s Sioux Falls had retained much of the attitude and posture that had been learned in the pioneer days. But it was changing ever so subtly. The pent-up demand for material things that the rest of the country was experiencing began to gnaw at its psyche and a new attitude was slowly acquired. No more scrimping and saving for tomorrow, tomorrow is here and 'I want to experience it now' was the new attitude. The Army Radio School northwest of town had closed and the 500 to 600 abandoned barracks were being sold and converted into businesses and housing. This still did not satisfy the demand for all of the required housing. Many of the young soldiers that had been trained at the air base returned to renew romances that they had generated during their short stay here. Marriages and families increased the demand for housing in the Heartland. But a new pattern was emerging. With the increased prosperity of the war, much more was being demanded by the returning defenders of freedom. Newer, faster, and flashier cars became the new mode of transportation. This increased the demand for better roads to drive them on, more service stations, more car-repair shops, and adequate parking facilities. Distances could be negotiated easier and homes were being built farther from the traditional central business district in the center of town.

With the lessons of World War II fresh in their minds, planners deducted that tract housing was the only way to build enough housing units to satisfy the pent-up demand. The eastern Hilltop Addition on the edge of the city where open farms had existed since the 1800s became converted to organized housing sites. The expansion and explosion of the City had began. No longer was the individual going to be left to his own direction, however. Planned communities were a necessity because so many people had to be accommodated at once. Wide, paved streets with curbs and gutters, city sewers, and city water, planned parks for recreation, and organized development of schools were bringing a subtle revolution of the community. No longer was the individual to be allowed to go his own way as had been pretty much the case since the European immigration began in the 1700s.

The prosperity that the Second World War had sparked was to also spark a new attitude in the people of the Heartland. No longer were they to be content with only black-colored cars and houses with furniture that was only functional. They wanted style and comfort. They were tired of the conservatism in their life. They wanted to let their hair down and change their conservative lifestyle. No longer would they continue to put up with the traditional direction their parents had forced on them. Too much had happened to them and their world. The new houses being built on the east side were only the first step in many changes to come. Along with this construction came needs for grocery stores, clothing stores, increased postal service, service stations, and other service industries that a community needs. The traditional downtown businesses had to make a move to the people or lose their business. Some adjusted, but many didn't. Many long-time traditional downtown businesses resisted the revolution because it was a subtle revolution that few understood.

The great influx of returning service men and the hope of prosperity fulfilled many but unfortunately too many were attracted to the city. This trend continues today. Before long the available jobs were taken and positions filled. It wasn't long before the realization that more jobs and money were needed to attain the 'good life' for those who wanted to work for it. For those full of the hope for the life that was promised in the advertisements on TV many small Heartland communities were resigned to disappointment. The prosperity was spotty and only attainable for a few. It was limited. There was not equality for all in this hope. These facts forced the continued exodus of many of the younger generation. Many of the younger generation had to leave the Heartland to obtain this prosperity.

*Happy trails to you............*

# *Order Form*

| TO PLACE AN ORDER: | | | |
|---|---|---|---|
| Quantity | Description | Price Each | Total |
| | *When Lilacs were in Bloom* | $12.95 | |
| | | Subtotal | |
| | | S.D. Residents add 6% S.D. Sales Tax | |
| | | Shipping and Handling | $3.00 |
| | | GRAND TOTAL | |

Name: ____________________

Address: ____________________

City____________ State _____ Zip Code _________

Phone: ____________________

*We Accept Mastercard, Visa, Check or Money Orders.*
*Send to:*

**RUSHMORE HOUSE PUBLISHING**
P.O. Box 1591
Sioux Falls, SD 57101
1-800-456-1895